# Forensic Psychotherapy
# and Psychopathology

Other titles in the
**Forensic Psychotherapy Monograph Series**

*Violence: A Public Health Menace and a Public Health Approach,*
  edited by Sandra L. Bloom

*Life within Hidden Worlds: Psychotherapy in Prisons,*
  edited by Jessica Williams Saunders

# Forensic Psychotherapy and Psychopathology
## Winnicottian Perspectives

edited by
*Brett Kahr*

Foreword by
*Vamık Volkan*

**Forensic Psychotherapy Monograph Series**

Series Editor
*Brett Kahr*

London & New York
KARNAC BOOKS

First published in 2001 by
H. Karnac (Books) Ltd.
6 Pembroke Buildings, London NW10 6RE

A subsidiary of Other Press LLC, New York

The views expressed in this book are the authors' own and do not necessarily reflect those of the Home Office and the Prison Department.

**British Library Cataloguing in Publication Data**

A C.I.P. for this book is available from the British Library

  ISBN: 1 85575 237 9

10 9 8 7 6 5 4 3 2 1

Edited, designed, and produced by Communication Crafts

www.karnacbooks.com

*Dedicated to the memory of my grandmother,*
*Dorothy Dorb Kahr*
*[1909–1994]*

"I suggest that in health there is a core to the personality."
Winnicott, 1963b, p. 187

"I find the inherited tendency cannot operate alone, and that in the developing baby and child it is the environment that facilitates individual growth."
Winnicott, 1969a, p. 186

# CONTENTS

vii

*Brett Kahr*

School of Psychotherapy and Counselling,
Regent's College, London

Throughout most of human history, our ancestors have done rather poorly when dealing with acts of violence. To cite but one of many shocking examples, let us perhaps recall a case from 1801, of an English boy aged only 13, who was executed by hanging on the gallows at Tyburn. What was his crime? It seems that he had been condemned to die for having stolen a spoon (Westwick, 1940).

In most cases, our predecessors have either *ignored* murderousness and aggression, as in the case of Graeco–Roman infanticide, which occurred so regularly in the ancient world that it acquired an almost normative status (deMause, 1974; Kahr, 1994); or they have *punished* murderousness and destruction with retaliatory sadism, a form of unconscious identification with the aggressor. Any history of criminology will readily reveal the cruel punishments inflicted upon prisoners throughout the ages, ranging from beatings and stockades, to more severe forms of torture, culminating in eviscerations, beheadings, or lynchings.

Only during the last one hundred years have we begun to develop the capacity to respond more intelligently and more humanely to acts of dangerousness and destruction. Since the advent of psychoanalysis, we now have access to a much deeper understanding both of the aetiology of aggressive acts and of their treatment; and nowadays we need no longer ignore criminals or abuse them—instead, we can provide compassion and containment, as well as conduct research that can help to prevent future acts of violence.

The modern discipline of forensic psychotherapy, which can be defined, quite simply, as the use of psychoanalytically orientated "talking therapy" to treat violent, offender patients, stems directly from the work of Sigmund Freud. Almost one hundred years ago, at a meeting of the Vienna Psycho-Analytical Society, held on 6 February 1907, Sigmund Freud anticipated the clarion call of contemporary forensic psychotherapists when he bemoaned the often horrible treatment of mentally ill offenders, in a discussion on the psychology of vagrancy. According to Otto Rank, Freud's secretary at the time, the founder of psychoanalysis expressed his sorrow at the "nonsensical treatment of these people in prisons" (quoted in Nunberg & Federn, 1962, p. 108).

Many of the early psychoanalysts preoccupied themselves with forensic topics. Hanns Sachs, himself a trained lawyer, and Marie Bonaparte, the French princess who wrote about the cruelty of war, spoke fiercely against capital punishment. Sachs, one of the first members of Freud's secret committee, regarded the death penalty for offenders as an example of group sadism (Moellenhoff, 1966). Bonaparte, who had studied various murderers throughout her career, had actually lobbied politicians in America to free the convicted killer Caryl Chessman, during his sentence on Death Row at the California State Prison in San Quentin, albeit unsuccessfully (Bertin, 1982).

Some years later, Melanie Klein concluded her first book, the landmark text *Die Psychoanalyse des Kindes* [*The Psycho-Analysis of Children*], with resounding passion about the problem of violence. Mrs Klein noted that acts of criminality invariably stem from disturbances in childhood, and that if young people could receive access to psychoanalytic treatment at any early age, then much cruelty could be prevented in later years. Klein expressed the hope that: "If every child who shows disturbances that are at all severe were to be analysed in good time, a great number of these people who later end up in prisons or lunatic asylums, or who go completely to pieces, would be saved from such a fate and be able to develop a normal life" (1932, p. 374).

Shortly after the publication of Klein's transformative book, Atwell Westwick, a Judge of the Superior Court of Santa Barbara,

California, published a little-known though highly inspiring article, "Criminology and Psychoanalysis" (1940), in the *Psychoanalytic Quarterly*. Westwick may well be the first judge to commit himself in print to the value of psychoanalysis in the study of criminality, arguing that punishment of the forensic patient remains, in fact, a sheer waste of time. With foresight, Judge Westwick queried, "Can we not, in our well nigh hopeless and overwhelming struggle with the problems of delinquency and crime, profit by medical experience with the problems of health and disease? Will we not, eventually, terminate the senseless policy of sitting idly by until misbehavior occurs, often with irreparable damage, then dumping the delinquent into the juvenile court or reformatory and dumping the criminal into prison?" (p. 281). Westwick noted that we should, instead, train judges, probation officers, social workers, as well as teachers and parents, in the precepts of psychoanalysis, in order to arrive at a more sensitive, non-punitive understanding of the nature of criminality. He opined: "When we shall have succeeded in committing society to such a program, when we see it launched definitely upon the venture, as in time it surely will be—then shall we have erected an appropriate memorial to Sigmund Freud" (p. 281).

In more recent years, the field of forensic psychotherapy has become increasingly well constellated. Building upon the pioneering contributions of such psychoanalysts and psychotherapists as Edward Glover, Grace Pailthorpe, Melitta Schmideberg, and more recently Murray Cox, Ismond Rosen, Estela Welldon, and others too numerous to mention, forensic psychotherapy has now become an increasingly formalized discipline that can be dated to the inauguration of the International Association for Forensic Psychotherapy and to the first annual conference, held at St. Bartholomew's Hospital in London in 1991. The profession now boasts a more robust foundation, with training courses developing in the United Kingdom and beyond. Since the inauguration of the Diploma in Forensic Psychotherapy (and subsequently the Diploma in Forensic Psychotherapeutic Studies), under the auspices of the British Postgraduate Medical Federation of the University of London in association with the Portman Clinic, students can now seek further instruction in the psychodynamic treatment of patients who act out in a dangerous and illegal manner.

The volumes in this series of books will aim to provide both practical advice and theoretical stimulation for introductory students

and for senior practitioners alike. In the Karnac Books Forensic Psychotherapy Monograph Series, we will endeavour to produce a
regular stream of high-quality titles, written by leading members of the
profession, who will share their expertise in a concise and practice-
orientated fashion. We trust that such a collection of books will help
to consolidate the knowledge and experience that we have already
acquired and will also provide new directions for the upcoming decades of the new century. In this way, we shall hope to plant the seeds
for a more rigorous, sturdy, and wide-reaching profession of forensic
psychotherapy.

As the new millennium begins to unfold, we now have an opportunity for psychotherapeutically orientated forensic mental health
professionals to work in close conjunction with child psychologists
and with infant mental health specialists so that the problems of
violence can be tackled both preventatively and retrospectively. With
the growth of the field of forensic psychotherapy, we at last have
reason to be hopeful that serious criminality can be forestalled and
perhaps, one day, even eradicated.

## References

Bertin, C. (1982). *La Dernière Bonaparte*. Paris: Librairie Académique
    Perrin.
deMause, L. (1974). The evolution of childhood. In: Lloyd deMause (Ed.),
    *The History of Childhood* (pp. 1–73). New York: Psychohistory Press.
Kahr, B. (1994). The historical foundations of ritual abuse: an excavation
    of ancient infanticide. In: Valerie Sinason (Ed.), *Treating Survivors of
    Satanist Abuse* (pp. 45–56). London: Routledge.
Klein, M. (1932). *The Psycho-Analysis of Children*, trans. Alix Strachey.
    London: Hogarth Press and The Institute of Psycho-Analysis. [First
    published as *Die Psychoanalyse des Kindes*. Vienna: Internationaler
    Psychoanalytischer Verlag.]
Moellenhoff, F. (1966). Hanns Sachs, 1881–1947: the creative uncon-
    scious. In: F. Alexander, S. Eisenstein, & M. Grotjahn (Eds.), *Psycho-
    analytic Pioneers* (pp. 180–199). New York: Basic Books.
Nunberg, H., & Federn, E. (Eds.) (1962). *Minutes of the Vienna Psychoana-
    lytic Society. Volume I: 1906–1908*, trans. Margarethe Nunberg. New
    York: International Universities Press.
Westwick, A. (1940). Criminology and Psychoanalysis. *Psychoanalytic
    Quarterly*, 9: 269–282.

# CONTRIBUTORS

**Donald Campbell** is a psychoanalyst and a child psychoanalyst, having trained at the Institute of Psycho-Analysis in London, and at the Hampstead Child-Therapy Clinic in London which has now become the Anna Freud Centre. He works as Consultant Child Psychotherapist at the Portman Clinic in London and as a Training Analyst at the Institute of Psycho-Analysis. He is the current President of the British Psycho-Analytical Society.

**Murray Cox** died on 28 June 1997. Before his death, he worked as a Consultant Psychotherapist at Broadmoor Hospital in Berkshire. The late Dr Cox held membership in the Group-Analytic Society, as well as Honorary Membership of the Institute of Group Analysis. He also served as Honorary Research Fellow of The Shakespeare Institute at the University of Birmingham, and as a Fellow of the Royal College of Psychiatrists. His many books include *Structuring the Therapeutic Process: Compromise with Chaos—The Therapist's Response to the Individual and the Group; Mutative Metaphors in Psychotherapy: The Aeolian Mode*, written with Alice Theilgaard; and the major two-volume textbook *Forensic Psycho-*

*therapy: Crime, Psychodynamics and the Offender Patient* (*Vol. I: Mainly Theory; Vol. II: Mainly Practice*), co-edited with Christopher Cordess.

**Em Farrell** is a psychotherapist. She serves as Director of the Free Associations Education Programme in London, and she maintains a private practice. She is a Visiting Faculty Member in the School of Psychotherapy and Counselling at Regent's College in London. She has written a book on the psychoanalytic psychotherapy of eating disorders, *Lost for Words: The Psychoanalysis of Anorexia and Bulimia*.

**Peter Giovacchini** is a psychiatrist and psychoanalyst and is Emeritus Clinical Professor of Psychiatry at the University of Illinois College of Medicine. He currently maintains a private psychoanalytic practice in Winnetka, Illinois. He has written many books on the treatment of borderline and psychotic patients, including *Treatment of Primitive Mental States*. Other books include *A Clinician's Guide to Reading Freud*, and *A Narrative Textbook of Psychoanalysis*.

**Jennifer Johns** trained in psychoanalysis at the Institute of Psycho-Analysis in London. She serves on the Winnicott Publications Committee and as the Chair of The Winnicott Trust. She edited the collected papers of her late father, Dr Thomas Main, *The Ailment and Other Psychoanalytic Essays*, and she has also co-edited a volume of Winnicott's papers, *Thinking About Children*, along with Ray Shepherd and Helen Taylor Robinson.

**Brett Kahr** works as Senior Lecturer in Psychotherapy in the School of Psychotherapy and Counselling at Regent's College in London, and as a Tutor in the Department of Primary Care and Population Sciences at the Royal Free and University College Medical School of the University of London. He is the author of *D. W. Winnicott: A Biographical Portrait*, which won the Gradiva Award for Biography. He is Patron of the Squiggle Foundation and Adviser to the Winnicott Clinic of Psychotherapy. He is Editorial Consultant for *The Psychotherapy Review*.

**Jeannie Milligan** trained as a social worker and then as an adult psychotherapist. She worked for ten years as a Social Worker at the Portman Clinic in London, specializing in the treatment of forensic patients and their families. She now works as Clinical Lecturer in Social Work in the Adolescent Department at the Tavistock Clinic.

**Joan Raphael-Leff** is a social psychologist and a psychoanalyst, and a graduate of the Institute of Psycho-Analysis in London. She is Professor of Psychoanalytic Studies at the University of Essex, and she has also served for many years as Deputy Editor of the *British Journal of Psychotherapy*. She has written two books in the field of perinatal psychology, *Psychological Processes of Childbearing* and *Pregnancy: The Inside Story*. She is also editor of *Spilt Milk: Perinatal Loss and Breakdown* and the co-editor, with Rosine Jozef Perelberg, of *Female Experience: Three Generations of British Psychoanalysts on Work with Women*.

**Valerie Sinason** is a child psychotherapist, a psychoanalyst, and a former teacher. She is the Clinical Director of the Clinic for Dissociative Studies. She is also an Honorary Consultant Child Psychotherapist at the University of Cape Town Child Guidance Clinic, South Africa, as well as Consultant Research Psychotherapist in the Department of the Psychiatry of Disability at St. George's Hospital Medical School in London. Her books include: *Mental Handicap and the Human Condition: New Approaches from the Tavistock, Treating Survivors of Satanist Abuse,* and *Memory in Dispute*. She has also published two volumes of poetry entitled *Inkstains and Stilettos* and *Night Shift*.

**Charles Socarides** maintains a private psychoanalytic practice in New York. He is also a Clinical Professor of Psychiatry at the Albert Einstein College of Medicine in New York City. He is well known for his many books, including *Homosexuality* and *The Preoedipal Origins and Psychoanalytic Therapy of Sexual Perversions*.

**Estela Welldon** works as Consultant Psychiatrist in Psychotherapy at the Portman Clinic in London, and she is a Fellow of the Royal College of Psychiatrists. She is the founding President of the International Association for Forensic Psychotherapy and serves as

Honorary Senior Lecturer in Forensic Psychotherapy at University College London. She is the author of *Mother, Madonna, Whore: The Idealization and Denigration of Motherhood* and also co-edited *A Practical Guide to Forensic Psychotherapy* with Cleo Van Velsen.

# ACKNOWLEDGEMENTS

I want to extend my very warmest thanks to the many talented and thoughtful clinicians who have contributed essays to this volume, all of whom I hold in great esteem. Sadly, since the commissioning of these articles, one of the contributors has passed away. On Saturday, 28 June 1997, my cherished teacher in forensic psychotherapy, Dr Murray Cox, died on the operating table while undergoing cardiac surgery. The news of Murray Cox's early death sent waves of shock and disbelief through the British mental health community. Many of us had enjoyed his effervescent company only two months earlier at the London meeting of the International Association for Forensic Psychotherapy, where he delivered a characteristically excellent paper, and he even regaled us with his superb piano playing at the conference banquet. I owe Murray Cox an everlasting debt of gratitude as the person who first encouraged me to embark upon forensic work. He accepted my invitation to contribute a chapter to this volume with eagerness, and he completed his sterling article on the secure hospital as a holding environment without any delay. He also waited patiently for the book to appear, and it saddens me that he did not live to see the final product. He has taught us all so much, and he will be much missed and much remembered, especially by his family, but also by his friends, his colleagues, his students, and his many patients, to whom he dedicated so much of himself over many long decades.

Not only do I wish to express my gratitude to the many contributors, but also to the excellent and efficient staff at Karnac Books, especially Cesare Sacerdoti and Graham Sleight, for their tremendous patience and interest throughout the long genesis of this project. Additionally, I must convey my appreciation to Paul Bunten and Dr George Makari, custodians of the Donald W. Winnicott Papers at The Oskar Diethelm Library of the History of Psychiatry in New York City, for permission to quote from a fragment of an unpublished letter from Donald Winnicott to Richard Balbernie.

I also wish to record my thanks to the staff and students at both the School of Psychotherapy and Counselling at Regent's College, and at the Tavistock Clinic, for their ongoing interest in my work. I owe a very special set of thanks to the staff of the Tate Library at Regent's College, and the staff at the Tavistock Clinic Library, for their continuously cheerful and intelligent assistance with a multitude of wide-ranging bibliographical enquiries over the years. In particular, I extend my appreciation to Anne Gorman, the head Librarian at Regent's College, and to Margaret Walker, the former Librarian at the Tavistock Clinic.

Brett Kahr
*Regent's Park, London*

# FOREWORD

*Vamık Volkan*

At the International Psychoanalytic Association's first Inter-Regional Conference meeting in Vienna in May 1998, I was once more powerfully reminded of Donald Winnicott's decisive influence on psychoanalysis. As this informal networking and "cross-pollination" session on "Transference and Its Impact on Education" progressed, I found myself startled by the sharp differences that arose between the colleagues who had gathered from parts of the world as far distant as Brazil and Britain, France and Argentina, Israel, Austria, and the United States. Though, of course, we all shared the basic concepts of classical psychoanalysis, our therapeutic techniques and theories ranged widely: some interpreted a patient's every statement, whereas others waited for the "storyline" of the transference neurosis to ripen before attempting interpretation; some referred to the abstract "father element" or "mother element" in teaching, sounding more philosophical than psychoanalytic, whereas others focused on clinical observations of how a particular student experienced his or her teacher as an oedipal mother or father. Influences varied with equal drama—colleagues from outside the United States regularly cited theoreticians whose work rarely figures in my own, and no participant in the conference mentioned the work of Margaret Mahler (1968), whose naturalistic observations have affected my thought and practice so deeply. In fact, other than Freud, there were very few thinkers who had influenced all of the participants of the Vienna conference. Donald Winnicott was one of these few thinkers.

In the tradition of the monumental 1978 volume *Between Reality and Fantasy: Transitional Objects and Phenomena*, edited by Simon Grolnick and Leonard Barkin in collaboration with Werner Muensterberger, the present book represents a major attempt to synthesize and to extend Winnicott's insights. Though editor Brett Kahr does not specifically cite *Between Reality and Fantasy* as a forerunner to this project, *Forensic Psychotherapy and Psychopathology: Winnicottian Perspectives* focuses Grolnick and Barkin's view of "the transitional process . . . as one of the basic organizing principles of the essential fabric of intrapsychic functioning" (Grolnick et al., 1978, p. xiii) on the specific problems of antisocial behaviour, individual violence, and criminal activity.

Though the contributions to this volume contemplate a variety of issues, they are united by Winnicott's (1953a) crucial formulations of transitional object, transitional space, and transitional relatedness; in its foundation on these concepts, this book shares a starting point with my own work on "magical" objects. Though the distinction between the transitional object and the adult fetish has been conclusively defined in the psychoanalytic literature (see, for example, Greenacre, 1969), the differences between the transitional object and other inanimate or non-human objects have not always been clearly maintained. Thus I have long been concerned with the misapplication of the transitional object concept. The transitional object (or phenomenon) allows the infant to develop, in response to the ministrations of the "good-enough" mother, "a temporary construction to aid . . . in the early stages of developing a sense of reality and establishing his own individual identity. It is of positive value in monitoring growth and expansion" (Greenacre, 1969, p. 334) and "does not generally forecast abnormal development" (p. 335). When the mother is not "good enough," however, the child develops a "psychotic preoccupation" with a bizarre inanimate object (which is not like a typical soft transitional object) such as a fan, a record player, or a jar (Mahler, 1968). These objects are properly called "childhood fetishes" or "psychotic fetishes," rather than "transitional objects," and they reflect a problem in the development of the normal transitional phase of life and early mother–child relationships.

I have also proposed two other "magical" objects with specific functions of their own belonging to phases of life different from that at which the transitional object normally appears: "linking objects" (Volkan, 1981; Volkan & Zintl, 1993) and "suitable reservoirs" (Volkan, 1988, 1997, 1999). The linking object is a site at which the representation of a lost object and the corresponding image of an adult mourner meet externally; as long as the linking object remains under the mourner's absolute control, the process of mourning is "frozen". Whereas the linking object generally incorporates symbolism, the original transitional object—and the one reactivated in adulthood—are protosymbols (Werner & Kaplan, 1963) which are to the individual what they ought to represent. The suitable reservoir, though it also appears in childhood, is discrete from the transitional object as well. Appearing around the age of 36 months, an age more advanced than that at which original transitional objects develop, the suitable reservoir serves in the development of large-group (e.g., racial or ethnic) identity as a repository for the child's unintegrated self- and object-images (for details, see Volkan, 1988, 1997, 1999). Interfering with the establishment of suitable reservoirs may cause difficulties in developing a solid large-group identity, as intruding on the development of transitional objects may cause problems in mental development. And, like transitional objects, adult versions of suitable reservoirs may be reactivated under conditions that are stressful for large-group identity. Whatever the structural similarities between transitional objects and other kinds of "magical" inanimate or non-human objects, however, it is essential to differentiate between them and between "normal" and pathological versions of each variety.

The contributions of this book are linked not only by Winnicott's theoretical foundation, but also by Winnicottian therapeutic techniques. Winnicott (1971) himself, for whom squiggle drawings were part of the daily routine, once wrote, "Playing is an experience, always a creative experience, and it is an experience in the space–time continuum, a basic form of living" (p. 30); we may now say, indeed, that play is not only a basic form of living, but also a basic form of psychotherapeutic treatment. The contributors to the present volume all engage in forms of creative play to treat patients whose abnormal development of transitional objects and violated transitional spaces have either led them to antisocial or criminal behaviour or put them at risk for such behaviour. And, like Winnicott, the contributors to the present volume have developed a number of therapeutically very useful metaphors—"pseudo-normality", "primary maternal persecution", and "vomit as transitional object" are just a few examples—to explain the workings of the forensic psychopathologies under consideration here. Such metaphors, I believe, help shift clinicians' focus from the overwhelming pathology to the matter that can be "played" with to treat patients most effectively.

Chapters that report recreating the transitional space between therapists and offenders (or sexual perverts), so that patients use their therapists as transitional objects, provide examples of such therapeutic "play". These authors observe that, in general, the offender (or pervert) perceives the transitional object as part of the self when it is perceived as soothing, and as external to the self when it is a target of his or her aggression. In the conventional understanding of transitional objects, space, and relatedness in development, the child has to perceive the transitional object both internally and externally and to be able to play with it in the transitional space long enough before he or she can move up the developmental ladder to form genuine object relations. "Similarly", as Peter Giovacchini (2000), a contributor to this volume, states elsewhere, "as patients make therapists into transitional objects, the transitional space is constructed and psychopathology is dealt with in that venue. As resolution occurs therapists again become part of the external world" (p. 267). The patient can then introject and identify with the ego functions of the therapist (who is now experienced as an external object in his or her own right), enriching the patient's mental life. I must add here that no therapy that corrects only a patient's deficiencies due to deprivation of "good-enough" mothering and related transitional object problems should be considered complete. The patient must move up to developmentally higher- (i.e., oedipal-) level phases within the transference neurosis and needs to experience phase-specific functioning in such levels for the first time with a newly modified and integrated self-representation. In other words, correcting early deficiencies should be supplemented with help for the patient's developmentally higher-level problems.

As Brett Kahr reminds us, forensic psychotherapy—a term coined several years ago by Estela Welldon, another contributor to the present volume—is a relatively recent development. Given Winnicott's own wish to train a substantial number of psychotherapists properly and thoroughly in order to contribute materially to the problem of treating offenders rather than simply punishing them, the creation of the International Association for Forensic Psychotherapy in 1991 and the establishment of the world's first diploma course in forensic psychotherapy in 1994 represent steps in the right direction. But it is important to recognize that there will—perhaps always, perhaps inevitably—be tensions between those whose first priority is to protect society and those whose first priority is to help the individual whose psychopathologies result in criminal and/or antisocial behaviour. Though, it can be argued, treating a criminal serves the society in which he or she lives by reforming the offender into a good (or at least harmless) citizen, criminal and/or antisocial behaviour may of course continue while the offender is in treatment, posing a dilemma for the psychotherapist or analyst as well as for the policymaker. I myself have confronted this dilemma in supervising the psychotherapy of a paedophile: initially, Dr William Greer of Norfolk, Virginia, and I were torn between the desire to treat this man and the desire to protect his community from his damaging conduct. In the end, our therapeutic identities gained the upper hand, and Dr Greer's treatment was successful (see the Dog Man case in Volkan, 1995). In other cases, however, the responsibility of protecting other members of the society in which the offender lives may be simply overwhelming.

The Institute of Law, Psychiatry and Public Policy at the Uni-versity of Virginia—of which I have been an Administrative Board member since the institute was founded in 1977—is a unique organization dedicated to finding a humane balance between these sometimes apparently incommensurate demands; by forging significant links between the schools of law and medicine, the institute connects therapeutic considerations and legal concerns.

The institute is not a clinic, but rather a social agent striving to create a public atmosphere supportive to the practice of forensic psychotherapy. A faculty that combines legal professionals and psychotherapists works to understand, prevent, and manage violence in society; to promote the human rights of persons who have or are perceived to have mental illnesses; to improve law and public policy related to child protection, legal responsibility, and related issues; and to provide reliable clinical information to courts so that the judicial system can make informed decisions regarding mental health issues. Indeed, many of the institute's programs can be seen as sister efforts to the child care and therapeutic activities described by several authors in this volume. Such interdisciplinary collaboration, I believe, will be crucial to the "preventive medicine" practised by those contributors to the present volume who treat children and youths with structural defects liable to develop antisocial behaviour or criminal intentions. By fostering public interest and policy debate, forensic psychotherapists can promote the very early childhood care that may prevent individual violence and antisocial or criminal activity—which, after all, must be our common goal not just as clinicians, but as citizens of the communities in which we live and work. This book is a solid stepping-stone in the process of establishing the parameters and potentials of this new field.

# Forensic Psychotherapy and Psychopathology

"The treatment of the antisocial tendency is not psycho-analysis. It is the provision of child care."

Winnicott, 1956b, p. 315

# Introduction

## Winnicott's contribution to the study of dangerousness

*Brett Kahr*

Since the inauguration of the International Association for Forensic Psychotherapy in 1991, and the creation of the world's first diploma course in forensic psychotherapy in 1994 under the joint auspices of the British Postgraduate Medical Federation of the University of London, and the Portman Clinic, the psychoanalytic study and treatment of both perverse and delinquent patients has become an increasingly visible and important area of expertise within the mental health field. Stirred on by the foundational work of Dr Estela Welldon, who first coined the term "forensic psychotherapy", this arena of study has become increasingly visible in recent years, and now, for the first time, the Royal College of Psychiatrists of the United Kingdom has created a specialist training in forensic psychotherapy for psychiatric registrars. After a long and continuous struggle, it has become much more possible for workers to offer *psychological treatment* to the offender-patient, rather than the proverbial *punishment*.

Although many of us derive great pleasure from the innovativeness and freshness of the newly constituted profession of forensic psychotherapy, we must not forget that the roots of psychoanalytic work with dangerous and perverse individuals reach back at least into the very early years of the last century. Sigmund Freud, the founder of psychoanalysis, would have had the opportunity to observe many violent and uncontained patients in the Allgemeines Krankenhaus on the outskirts of Vienna; and though Freud did not focus on forensic patients as such, he did treat at least one paedophile patient (Kahr, 1999, in preparation), and he provided supervision for a paedophile patient under the care of his student Theodor Reik (Kahr, 1991, in preparation; Natterson, 1966). Sigmund Freud maintained an extremely sympathetic attitude to forensic matters, and in his letter to the convicted felon Georg Fuchs, Freud lamented the horrific punishments meted out to prisoners, which Freud himself regarded as "a manifestation of the brutality and the folly that dominate present civilized mankind" (quoted in Eissler, 1961, p. 199).

Freud also wrote an important essay on psychoanalysis and criminology, entitled "Psycho-Analysis and the Establishment of the Facts in Legal Proceedings" (1906b), as well as an article on "Some Character-Types Met with in Psycho-Analytic Work" (1916d), which contains the memorable section entitled "Criminals from a Sense of Guilt", in which he first espoused the notion that criminality begins in the phantasy life of the patient and that unconscious *ideas* lurk at the base of deviant behaviour. By underscoring the notion that delinquency stems from motivational causes, Freud provided us with the bedrock of subsequent theories in forensic psychotherapy. Sadly, Freud himself missed out on what may well have proved to be the most exciting piece of forensic consultation work. In 1924, Freud received an invitation to serve as a well-remunerated expert witness in the highly publicized American murder case in which two young men from Chicago, Nathan Leopold and Richard Loeb, stood trial for a brutal slaying. For reasons that remain not entirely clear to biographers, Freud refused to cooperate in the trial, despite the offer of a fee of $25,000 (Jones, 1957).

Other important works by Freud on forensically related matters include his little-known essay on "The Acquisition and Control of Fire" (1932a), which provides material on the psychogenesis of arson and pyromania. Freud also wrote insightfully about male homosexuality (1910c, 1911c [1910]), and female homosexuality (1920a), beating experiences (1919e), fetishism (1927e), parricide (1928b), and many other topics besides (cf. 1925f, 1931d).

Donald Winnicott has provided us with an extremely useful assessment of Freud's contribution to the study of forensic topics. In his classic essay "Psycho-Analysis and the Sense of Guilt", delivered in honour of Freud's centenary, Winnicott (1958a) wrote that, "More than anyone else it was Freud who paved the way for the understanding of antisocial behaviour and of crime as a *sequel* to an unconscious criminal intention, and a symptom of a failure in child-care" (pp. 31–32). Indeed, Winnicott's crisp summary aptly highlights the major ideas espoused by Freud—namely, that crime and perversion begin in the nursery.

Winnicott derived great inspiration from the work of Freud, and he even dedicated his book on children's medicine to Professor Freud (Winnicott, 1931) in gratitude. In the pages that follow, I shall undertake an examination of the ideas of Dr Donald Woods Winnicott [1896–1971], one of the most prolific and seminal pioneers of forensic psychotherapy, whose contribution to the field of delinquency remains of lasting value for practitioners of mental health.

Born in Plymouth in the county of Devon on 7 April 1896, Winnicott will undoubtedly be best remembered for his incomparable work in the field of infant mental health and child psychotherapy (Kahr, 1996a, 1996b, 2000). But Winnicott also wrote extensively and prolifically about a variety of forensic subjects, and it seems only fitting to pay tribute to this work. After a lengthy formation in the natural sciences at Jesus College of the University of Cambridge, followed by medical studies at St. Bartholomew's Hospital in London, Winnicott became a specialist in children's medicine. By 1924, he realized that he would have to undergo psychoanalytic training if he wished to provide comprehensive medico-psychological treatment for his many child patients at the Paddington Green Children's Hospital. After consulting with Dr Ernest Jones, the president of the British Psycho-Analytical Society, Winnicott embarked on a ten-year personal analysis with James Strachey, a Bloomsbury habitué who had only recently returned from an analysis with Freud in Vienna.

By 1934, Winnicott had qualified as a psychoanalyst of adult patients, and in 1935 he received his certification as a psychoanalyst of children. Even by this relatively early date in his career, Winnicott had already started to work with violent patients. More than twenty years later, Winnicott (1956b) would recall his first child training patient thus:

> For my first child analysis I chose a delinquent. This boy attended regularly for a year and the treatment stopped because of the disturbance that the boy caused in the clinic. I could say that the analysis was going well, and its cessation caused distress both to the boy and to myself in spite of the fact that on several occasions I got badly bitten on the buttocks. The boy got out on the roof and also he spilt so much water that the basement became flooded. He broke into my locked car and drove it away in bottom gear on the self-starter. The clinic ordered termination of the treatment for the sake of the other patients. He went to an approved school. [p. 306]

He continued to develop his forensic work in a variety of settings, most particularly during the Second World War, when he served as a consultant psychiatrist to the Government Evacuation Scheme, advising staff members of residential hostels, strewn throughout the Oxfordshire countryside, about the management of severely psychotic and delinquent children, many of whom had lost one or both parents during the Blitz on London. All in all, Winnicott maintained psychiatric responsibility for some 285 children, who made quite a nuisance of themselves by terrorizing the local townspeople, setting fire to hayricks, running away, and so forth (Winnicott & Britton, 1944, 1947). The staff became easily demoralized from caring for such abused and abusing children, most of whom suffered from the "double traumatization" of having already come from difficult backgrounds and then succumbed to the terrors of war. Winnicott provided indispensable supervision. According to Clare Winnicott (1984), formerly Clare Britton, the psychiatric social worker in charge of the hostels, "These sessions with him were the highlight of the week and were invaluable learning experiences for us all including Winnicott, who kept careful records of each child's situation and the stresses put on staff members. His comments were nearly always in the form of questions which widened the discussion and never violated the vulnerability of individual members" (p. 3).

According to contemporary psychoanalytic terminology, I suppose that we could describe Winnicott as a man who possessed a very finely developed "digestive capacity"—in other words, the ability to tolerate potent affects that other people might ignore or defend against. For instance, on 3 March 1943, Dr Elizabeth Rosenberg, a psychiatrist and psychoanalyst, presented a paper to an evening meeting of the British Psycho-Analytical Society on the war neuroses (Rosenberg, 1943). During the talk, an air-raid siren began to blare quite loudly, but the psychoanalysts seemed to pay no attention to the potential external danger. According to Dr Margaret Little, an eyewitness on that particular occasion, Winnicott rose to his feet, and called out, "I should like to point out that there is an air-raid going on" (quoted in Little, 1985, p. 19). He then suggested that the assembled company ought to walk downstairs to the air-raid shelter, but nobody responded to Winnicott's suggestion, and Dr Rosenberg continued to deliver her paper. As a source of inspiration to all good forensic practitioners, Winnicott proved able to tolerate the painful, external reality of the Blitz and to recommend appropriate managerial action.

Winnicott developed his psychoanalytic practice throughout the 1940s and 1950s, and he soon became one of the most respected psychoanalytic clinicians and thinkers in the country, renowned for his capacity to work with unbearable patients. In the course of writing a biography of Winnicott (Kahr, 1996a), I had the opportunity to meet many of Winnicott's former analytical patients; it soon became quite apparent that the vast majority had had previous, unsatisfactory experiences of psychotherapy or psychoanalysis with other practitioners, most of whom seemed incapable of helping the more distressed patient. In the tradition of many good forensic workers, Winnicott possessed the capacity to be simultaneously concerned as well as unfazed or unfrightened by his more disturbed and vulnerable patients, and his reputation for dealing with those who could not find help elsewhere soon grew and grew. Winnicott eventually rose to the rank of president of the British Psycho-Analytical Society, serving two terms, first from 1956 until 1959, and then again from 1965 until 1968. He died at his home in Belgravia, in southwest London, on 25 January 1971 at the age of 74.

Although Winnicott never worked in a traditional forensic setting, such as a prison or a medium-secure unit, he sustained a lively interest in forensic topics throughout his long clinical career. Not only did he work extensively with antisocial children and adolescents (Kahr, 1996b; Winnicott, 1956b), but he worked closely with the legal profession and with the probation service as well. For example, in 1967, he spoke to the Borstal Assistant Governors' Conference at King Alfred's College in Winchester, delivering his peerless paper on "Delinquency as a Sign of Hope" (1968), which eventually appeared in the *Prison Service Journal*, read by many probation officers.

A mere glance at the published volume of his selected correspondence (Winnicott, 1987) reveals ample evidence of Winnicott's continuous interest in forensic issues and concerns. In an intelligent letter, written to the Editor of *The Times*, Winnicott (1949b) pontificated about juvenile crime and about the management of Holloway Gaol, referring to the "knotty problem of crime and insanity". He further reflected that, "It is very seldom that the comments of a psychoanalyst are asked for or printed; instead it is assumed that the psychologist has an attitude, probably a sentimental one. The idea that psychoanalysis has no attitude, but that it can enlighten, seldom percolates" (p. 15). Through his frequent letters to politicians, ministers, and newspapers, Winnicott worked hard in his spare time in an attempt to enlighten public attitudes towards crime, emphasizing that psychoanalysis might make a very important contribution to the debate around working with highly distressed individuals. In that same letter, Winnicott (1949b) reminded his reader that we must not only consider the origins of crime, but also the fact that "there is another half of every antisocial act to be considered—society's revenge feelings" (p. 16), suggesting that much punishment stems from unconscious revenge on the part of the rest of us who have not committed overt criminal acts.

On 1 September 1949, Winnicott addressed two separate letters to government ministers, arguing to R. S. Hazlehurst that, "Stealing has practically no more relation to poverty and want than civil murder has to persecution" (Winnicott, 1949c, p. 17), and to S. H. Hodge that criminals actually suffer from psychological problems (Winnicott, 1949d), both of which were pioneering concepts in

Great Britain in the immediate postwar period. Amid the zeal of punishing those who perpetrate crimes, Winnicott represented a voice of particular humanity, urging that both psychiatric patients and criminals alike deserve the right to successful psychothera-peutic treatment.

Winnicott discovered a simultaneously gentle and firm means of becoming an agitator for the field of forensic psychopathology. In his communication to Dr P. D. Scott, a well-known consultant psychiatrist at the Maudsley Hospital, Winnicott (1950b) reflected that, "There is no doubt whatever that even if our knowledge of the psychopathology of criminology were to be complete tomor-row, there would still be a very great number of years before psychotherapists could be properly trained in numbers sufficient to make a practical difference to the problem" (p. 23). But he re-mained optimistic that such work could be undertaken, and he even chided his mentor, Melanie Klein, and their colleagues within the British Psycho-Analytical Society for having neglected to study the psychology of delinquency in sufficient detail (Winnicott, 1952; cf. Winnicott, 1948b, 1953b).

Above all, Winnicott drew upon his unique wealth of clinical experience to alert us to the fact that delinquency results from deprivation in early infancy and childhood. We have yet to grap-ple with the implications of this important concept, outlined most clearly in his pivotal essay "The Antisocial Tendency" (Winnicott, 1956b; cf. Winnicott, 1943, 1945, 1948a, 1949a, 1956b, 1960a, 1961b, 1963c). Beginning with the case of a young boy called "John", a lad who engaged in compulsive stealing from shops, Winnicott traced a theory in which he hypothesized that stealing represents not only an aggressive act towards the object, but also something rather *hopeful*, an indication that the child realizes that something has gone missing—usually parental love—and that the act of theft can serve as a means of attempting to compensate for early, lost psychic nutrients. Cleverly, Winnicott described how he had en-listed the cooperation of John's mother so that she could better understand the roots of her young son's offending behaviour. Winnicott explained to John's mother:

> "Why not tell him that you know that when he steals he is not
> wanting the things that he steals but he is looking for some-
> thing that he has a right to: that he is making a claim on his

mother and father because he feels deprived of their love." I
told her to use language which he could understand. [Winni-
cott, 1956b, p. 307]

John's mother absorbed Winnicott's thinking on this matter, and
she attempted to discuss the problem with her son. She wrote to
Winnicott some time later:

"I told him that what he really wanted when he stole money
and food and things was his mum; and I must say I didn't
really expect him to understand, but he did seem to. I asked
him if he thought we didn't love him because he was so
naughty sometimes, and he said right out that he didn't think
we did, much. Poor little scrap! I felt so awful, I can't tell you."
[quoted in Winnicott, 1956b, p. 307]

But Winnicott always encouraged patients to engage in verbaliza-
tion rather than enactment. Indeed, when Richard Balbernie, a
colleague from the child mental health field, wrote to Winnicott
enquiring whether foul language should be tolerated in children,
Winnicott (1969b) replied, "How much nicer is hate than murder
and how silly we are if we mind when children scream out 'fuck'
and other obscenities" (cf. Kahr, 1998).

Winnicott established an overt aetiological link between deprivation and delinquency, and he expressed the view that if we
manage to intervene early in childhood situations, then the prog-
nosis will be very good indeed. However, mindful of the fact that
many cases of seemingly intractable criminality and psychopathology do present themselves in adulthood, workers often become
depressed and despondent, particularly when confronted with
deeply entrenched behaviour. For this very reason, Winnicott
wrote his remarkable paper "Delinquency as a Sign of Hope"
(1968), encouraging workers to respond with reliability to delinquents, to help provide for something that could not be offered in
the early, maturational years.

Winnicott's contributions to the field of forensic psychotherapy
and to the study of severe psychopathology deserve a book-length
treatment, and a lifetime's study. One will be very hard-pressed
indeed to summarize the essence of Winnicott's fifty years as a
health care professional, from the time of his qualification as a
medical doctor in 1920 until his death in 1971. It remains my hope

that students will find themselves drawn to read Winnicott's texts for the first time, and that experienced practitioners will return to Winnicott's publications, as sources of inspiration and elucidation, and above all, compassion, for the deeply turbulent patients who often enter our consulting-rooms.

The essays in this volume, written by some of the most thoughtful of psychoanalytic practitioners, provide ample evidence of the ways in which Winnicott's rich clinical legacy has had a direct impact upon the work of contemporary mental health care professionals. Jennifer Johns, a member of the Winnicott Publications Committee and the Chair of The Winnicott Trust, offers us, in "Winnicott: A Beginning", an extremely clear guide to the main events within Winnicott's career. In her chapter, "Babies as Transitional Objects", Estela Welldon not only draws upon Winnicott's writings on the transitional object but continues, with his as yet under-appreciated work on maternal death wishes (Winnicott, 1949a), to explore the ways in which mothers can use and abuse their babies as objects and as receptacles for their own wishes and needs. In a similar spirit, in "Primary Maternal Persecution", Joan Raphael-Leff has elaborated upon her original concept—an alternative conceptualization to Winnicott's more antiseptic notion of "primary maternal preoccupation"—exploring the often fraught relationship between mothers and their infants. Valerie Sinason, in her chapter, "Children Who Kill Their Teddy Bears", provides a chilling contribution to the study of the perversion of motherhood, describing her pioneering work with the survivors of satanist rituals and other forms of grotesque abuse.

In her chapter, "Deprivation and Delinquency in the Treatment of the Adolescent Forensic Patient", Jeannie Milligan has offered us a moving case history that richly illustrates Winnicott's clinical observations and helpfully demonstrates the ways in which Winnicott's clinical concepts can have an immediate impact within the course of a psychotherapy session. Donald Campbell has introduced a new mechanism of defence into the literature with his chapter, "On Pseudo-Normality: A Contribution to the Psychopathology of Adolescence", describing how certain patients use highly defensive and ultimately unhelpful psychic strategies to ward off the pain of their personal predicament. In her chapter, "Vomit as a Transitional Object", Em Farrell has drawn upon her wealth of experience in the treatment of anorexic and bulimic individuals to expand on Winnicott's work on infantile feeding disturbances. Influenced in part by some of his personal contact with Winnicott in the 1960s, Peter Giovacchini, one of the seminal figures in the treatment of severely psychotic and borderline individuals, has explored the role of transitional objects in the treatment of primitive mental states in his chapter by the same title. Charles Socarides has undertaken an ambitious theoretical and clinical task in his contribution, "D. W. Winnicott and the Understanding of Sexual Perversions", exploring how so many of Winnicott's ideas will help to elucidate the often enmeshed dynamics between parents and infants that result in sexual perversions in later life. In the final chapter, "On the Capacity for Being Inside Enough", the late Murray Cox has bequeathed to us a beautiful essay on the importance of the holding environment in the residential rehabilitation of the forensic patient.

* * *

Before he died, Winnicott began to work on an autobiography, which he never managed to complete, entitled *Not Less Than Everything*. On the very opening page, Winnicott inscribed the following plea: "Oh God! May I be alive when I die" (quoted in C. Winnicott, 1978, p. 19). Although Winnicott could not survive his own mortality, his ideas continue to remain as vibrant as ever, and they provide us with many areas of assistance in the ongoing task of trying to treat and rehabilitate those suffering from psychosis or personality disorders. I trust that *Forensic Psychotherapy and Psychopathology: Winnicottian Perspectives* will serve as a source of clinical sustenance to those of us who have committed ourselves to this continuously challenging field of clinical endeavour.

# CHAPTER ONE

# Winnicott: a beginning

*Jennifer Johns*

It would require more than a single chapter to do any justice at all to Donald Winnicott's life and his contributions to the understanding of the developing inner world of the baby and child, his view of the importance of relationships in that development, and the continuing story of the vicissitudes of human life both as they affect and are affected by the developing individual. Winnicott's biography can be studied in the books about his work by Adam Phillips (1988) and Michael Jacobs (1995). Recently, Brett Kahr (1996a) has produced impressive details of his life. To summarize: Winnicott came from a stable English background that existed one hundred years ago, before the earthquakes of this century that were to affect both him and his work later.

Winnicott was the youngest child, the only boy, of a prosperous Methodist middle-class family with a strong sense of civic responsibility, living in Plymouth. He was sent to school in Cambridge, and then he later went to the University of Cambridge and studied biological sciences, before going to London to become a doctor. The son was special in a rather feminine family—his earnest father is described as being absent much of the time—with both the rewards and the burdens of specialness and responsibility. Going

11

away to school seems to have been something of a relief and perhaps allowed room for his playfulness and the music that he loved all his life.

At school, he read Charles Darwin, and he was excited by the ideas of natural selection, those complex interactions between environment and heredity that are responsible for shaping the natural world. This interest seems to have foreshadowed and influenced both his capacity for detailed observation and his later understanding of the delicate interaction of environment and inborn elements in the development of the individual human being.

In 1914, at 18 years of age, he saw his stable world plunged into destruction. At least five of his contemporaries from school were killed in the Great War, and he also lost university friends (Kahr, 1996a). In the military hospitals in Cambridge, as a student, he would have come across the wounded, gangrenous, maimed, gassed, and shell-shocked from the trenches, and he later saw action himself in the Royal Navy as a Surgeon Probationer on a destroyer. Following this exposure to trauma, he went to London to further his medical studies, and by 1919 he had discovered another great influence—Sigmund Freud and psychoanalysis. In particular, he relished *The Interpretation of Dreams* (1900a), Freud's major piece of writing before the introduction of the structural model, when the term "ego" meant much what we mean by the word "self" today.

With the influences of Darwin and Freud inside him, Winnicott qualified in medicine in 1920, and by 1923 he had become a specialist in paediatrics. He practised both in Hackney and at the Paddington Green Children's Hospital, where he remained for forty years, dealing with over twenty thousand cases, a volume of observational work unequalled by any other psychoanalyst. In 1923, Winnicott also married, and shortly thereafter he began his own personal analysis with James Strachey. He trained as an analyst from 1927 to 1934, during which time he published his first book, *Clinical Notes on Disorders of Childhood* (Winnicott, 1931). The book is now out of print, but it is quite remarkable for its careful descriptions of the physical examination and diagnosis of the sick child, as well as for its sensitivity to the emotional aspects of ill-health in children.

By 1935, Winnicott had also become a child psychoanalyst, having had supervision with Melanie Klein, his next great influence. By the time the Second World War broke out, he was a respected member of both the medical establishment and the British Psycho-Analytical Society. This "foot in both camps"—being both paediatrician and psychoanalyst—gave him the practical background to write and to broadcast widely on matters to do with the welfare of children and families. He spoke of early development, growth, feeding, school, siblings, the evacuation of children during the war, and the effects of separation from parents and subsequent difficulties, particularly delinquency. His information and ideas proved useful to parents, teachers, social workers, probation officers, doctors, and all students of human nature.

At the outset of the war, together with John Bowlby and Emanuel Miller, he had warned publicly of the dangers of the evacuation policy; their predictions came true in terms of the many children separated from their home environment who became distressed, difficult, and delinquent, requiring serious help and management (Bowlby, Miller, & Winnicott, 1939). It was while working with these children that Winnicott met another of his life's great influences, his colleague Clare Britton, a social worker, who later became his second wife. At that time, he also began the major part of his writing.

During the Second World War, there was internal conflict in the British psychoanalytic world, to do with the differing theories of early psychic development held by Anna Freud and by Melanie Klein. These controversies had a subsequent effect on Winnicott's psychoanalytic career, and he attended the famous Controversial Discussions. Winnicott, having been trained by Klein, became unable to align himself with her to the degree that she wished in relation to her theories about the inner world of the baby. Having observed so many babies and children with their mothers, he also valued Anna Freud's ideas about the internal world of the toddler and older child, and he had his own ideas about the earliest stages of life, finding it difficult to accept that the internal world of an infant could be so necessarily conflictual and persecuted as Klein believed. Winnicott, in no sense a "joiner", took neither side. He was a person who would question received knowledge, who could be challenging, even aggressive, to thinking that he regarded as wrong, or which was being used in a defensive way.

Besides, for Winnicott, during that war and the period of post-war austerity including the beginnings of the Welfare State, there were other things to do than engage closely in these debates. As well as responding to the public issues of the time about the effects of the emergency on children and families, his own observation of mothers and babies in clinics continued. A beautiful early example is the description of the baby's exploration of the set situation with the spatula, written in 1941, strengthening the foundations of his unique view of the earliest stages of individual development (Winnicott, 1941).

The dual focus of paediatrics and psychoanalysis is crucial to the understanding of Winnicott's work. He started as a paediatrician, a body doctor who knew that babies live in and are their bodies. There is no split between body and mind for them. Skin, joints, and feeling, eyes and vision, ears and hearing, orifices and gut lining, genitals, limbs, and excitement—these both produce and express affect and the beginnings of thought and being. Out of this he became concerned with the way babies become themselves, how they develop their own sense of being. For him, the crucial question was how they come to know that they are persons, which they do in relation to their mothers—one aspect of the facilitating environment. He approached and refined his views on this topic from many angles throughout his life.

Winnicott held that no two babies are the same, and that each mother–baby couple is unique. He believed that most human beings are born with what he called a maturational tendency towards growth and differentiation, given a more or less ordinary environment, and that an aspect of this was the tendency also to repair, given the facilitating environment. He described how, from the baby's point of view, awareness of separateness and individuality comes gradually out of a state of undifferentiation, in parallel with awareness of mother's separateness, and also in parallel with a sense of integration, all based on repeated experiences of body care, holding, nursing, gazing, exchange of vocalization. He observed that mothers and babies are always together, that one cannot be considered without the other, as encapsulated in his famous saying: "There's no such thing as a baby." He saw ordinary mothers unconsciously and in a bodily and psychological way adapting themselves to their babies, and he noted that pregnancy itself, with its enormous physiological and emotional changes, automatically lays the foundation for this primary maternal preoccupation. And he observed that normally the adaptation to the baby falters, becomes less perfect, in step with the baby's growing capacity to survive these failures. He called this process of attunement and its gradual loss "good-enough mothering".

Winnicott saw that as development proceeds and the difference between the baby's awareness of "me" and "not-me" strengthens, many babies need a link, a way of bridging the gap that might be too much for them, and he explained the existence of transitional phenomena, the use of a comforting blanket or teddy, or even a sound or thought. The transitional space in which such phenomena occur provides room for the development of play and also of the ability to stand separateness for increasing amounts of time.

Like all medical theorizing about health and normal development, inferences have to be drawn from states where that development has failed or has been interfered with, and Winnicott's observations were often of mother–baby couples where a "good-enough" environment had not been achieved—for instance, where a mother is absent, physically or emotionally, or is disturbed or intrusive, or when a particular baby has needs that cannot be fulfilled. One variety of "not good-enough" mother, when a mother cannot respond sensitively to what Winnicott describes as the baby's gesture, but substitutes one of her own, may result in the baby who cannot be spontaneous, only compliant or imitative. Such people have what he called a "false self". Such individuals may apparently lead successful lives, but at the price of their own vitality. He also wrote about the effect of mother's unconscious states, including her unconscious hatred of her baby, and he linked this with the hatred that those responsible for delinquents can come to feel towards their charges (cf. Winnicott, 1949a).

Winnicott's double and intertwined career continued, and in the 1950s and 1960s he was increasingly recognized, both in the paediatric world and in that of psychoanalysis and child psychiatry. He became a president of the Paediatric Section of the Royal

Society of Medicine, and of the Association of Child Psychology and Psychiatry, among many other honours. Until his death in 1971, he continued to write about many subjects, such as play, the child's sense of morality, adolescence, juvenile delinquency, and his own communication with children, both his clinical accounts and the use of the squiggle game—at every step refining his view of human development. Also concerned with social issues and contemporary matters such as adolescent problems, democracy, or the atomic bomb, he addressed national and international audiences of varying degrees of sophistication, and he always wrote according to his audience, whoever it contained.

At the time of his death, Winnicott had published a little over half of his work. Clare Winnicott became the driving spirit behind the publication of much of the remainder, aided by Madeleine Davis and Ray Shepherd. Later, realizing the approach of her own death, Clare Winnicott set up The Winnicott Trust, for two purposes: firstly, to complete the work of publication; secondly, to further the links between the world of psychoanalysis and other spheres, especially paediatrics and child psychiatry. The Winnicott Trust, originally under the chairmanship of the late Dr Martin James, and subsequently of Dr Jonathan Pedder and, more recently, myself, has been active in promoting the work of Professor Lynne Murray and her colleagues at the Winnicott Research Unit at the University of Cambridge, and it has also provided funds for other research, including that of Professor Peter Hobson at the Tavistock Clinic in London.

This can only be a short account of this small, at first meeting insignificant-looking man, with his high-pitched voice and wicked sense of humour, who has influenced our world so greatly. His own description of himself, given to a child psychiatric conference shortly before his death, includes the following words:

> Among other things was always the fact that I am rather an ordinary person, neurotic along the English inhibited pattern, at one time being inordinately shy, and not quite so tall as I intended to be, which I have always felt to be a major fault. I spent the first two decades of my life half-drowned in a perpetual sense of guilt, from which psychoanalysis rescued me, except that I can never escape from the sense that I ought not to

have escaped the death that eclipsed the careers of so many of my friends in the 14–18 War. [Winnicott, 1970]

Donald Winnicott escaped that death, but he spent his life studying the ways in which persons achieve life, a sense of liveliness, and ongoing being. His ideas survive, and they are carried on by workers whom he never met, in fields he might not have thought of, but whom he would have enjoyed, argued with, and, from my own memories and what we know of him, probably been troublesome to.

# CHAPTER TWO

# Babies as transitional objects

*Estela Welldon*

I saw a man who had requested a consultation with a female psychiatrist. The first time he came, he asked me directly and emphatically: "Are you Jewish or Catholic?" Although the question did not take me by surprise, since patients or prospective patients would like to know all sorts of information regarding their psychotherapists, the tone of this man's question conveyed a sense of urgency and despair that made me feel that it was necessary to take into account its deeper, unconscious layers. As usual, I explained that, though the factual information could be easily imparted, this would immediately pre-empt access to other immensely significant areas unknown to himself that could give us important clues to his present predicament.

This patient was a married man in his mid-40s with four children who had referred himself with the following letter:

"I have lived with a condition for most of my life which manifests itself in the form of transvestial [*sic*] or transsexual behaviour and feelings. Whilst I am able to suppress these feelings for a good deal of the time, there nevertheless comes a moment when I can cope no longer—has happened now [. . .] and for the first time self-mutilation seems to be logical. [. . .] *I desperately need someone to help me* decide upon the best way in which I could free myself of my now unremitting torment. [. . .] The symptoms that I am experiencing at the moment fall into two quite distinct categories, i.e. mental and physical. Mentally, I feel that I am a woman in the cliché situation of having to masquerade my way through life simply because I am not as perfect as I want to be. [. . .] I can quite see the clear possibilities of a "change". To this end I have now almost cut myself off emotionally from those around me—and so the conflict rages, as I question: to whom does my first loyalty lie, my family, all of whom are and will be able to make lives of their own, or to myself, with one precious life only? [. . .] On the physical side, the tension can only be relieved by wearing anything other than men's clothes. [. . .] More obvious symptoms, physical side that is, are: morning sickness, vomiting through the day, loss of appetite, feeling shivery, aching in the small of the back and the most obvious sign that tells me when I am about to "go under" again—that my breasts become tender and sore—and it is at these times that the sensation of my nipples touching against my woolly jumper makes me just want to scream. [. . .]"

The letter continued in the same vein. From his own description of his problem, we can vividly experience his enormous despair and his sense of despondency and desolation.

He told me of his bizarre and complicated early childhood. He was the younger child in a family of two, with an older sister. When he was 1 year old, during the Second World War, he was sent to stay with one of his aunts for "reasons of safety". His early recollections had to do with feelings of being lost. He remembered his time with his aunt as an extremely confused one. She was a warm and kind woman, but suddenly, when he was aged 3, she made it blatantly clear to him that unless he complied with all her wishes, she would withdraw her love. The conditions she imposed included not only wearing girl's clothes, but behaving like a girl as well. He still remembers with trepidation that period of his life. At the beginning, he tried to go against his aunt's whims, but he soon realized that the consequence would be complete isolation. After all, he had already been given away by his own mother, from whom he received a few postcards, but never a visit. He then started to comply with everything required of him. After an initial period of resistance during which he felt awkward, uneasy, and on the alert lest others should notice his being a "fraud", his mood changed, and he acquired a growing sense of self-confidence while wearing girls' dresses. Actually, to his own surprise, he began to thoroughly enjoy this "imposed" cross-dressing, when everyone took it for granted that he was a girl.

Tellingly, his aunt had had a daughter, who had died at a very early age, and this was followed shortly afterwards by her husband's death. The aunt now decided to send her nephew to an all-girls school, and she taught him how to behave like a girl; for medical visits, she would come to London and have him examined by a doctor friend of hers. At the age of 12, he looked convincingly like a girl. On the occasion of a family member's wedding, he was made the bridesmaid. He became the object of the most extraordinary scandal when, during the ceremony, his real mother—who had not seen him since she had sent him to live with his aunt—suddenly realized that this beautiful "girl" who was accompanied by "her" aunt was in fact her own son. Amid screams and shouts, he was taken away by his real mother, who not only severely punished him, but proceeded immediately to send him to an all-boys school. There, his suffering, torment, and humiliation became so great that eventually his mother decided to send him back to his aunt, but things were never to be as they had been before. He now had to suffer his aunt's denigration for his "maleness". I prefer not to go any further into this case here. What has been said will be sufficient to convey the horrors that the two women, in their role of mother, together inflicted on this poor boy from infancy to adolescence.

But what about his first question to me? His father and mother were Jewish, but the aunt, who had been married to the brother of the boy's father and who had brought the boy up since the age of

1 year, was the only Catholic member of his family. He had been surrounded by all sorts of "maternal" perverting attitudes throughout his early life, both from his mother and from his aunt. The fact that I did not give him any information about my personal life—in this case, my religious affiliation—gave us the chance to explore his trepidation in his own search for who he really was. Had I been Jewish, would it have implied for him that I wanted him to *continue* to be a male? But, if, on the other hand, I had been a Catholic, would he have felt forced to go ahead with *his* trans-sexual wish? Would he have felt free enough to wonder about the intricacies of his own gender identity, or indeed to look into his own sense of anger and confusion created by the two women carers in his early life? He had been messed about, forced to take up being neither a boy nor a girl, not only to please both women but also to secure not only his psychological but also his physical survival. In an earlier work (Welldon, 1988), I argued that mother-hood plays a key role in the aetiology of perversion and that, for some women, motherhood could provide an excellent vehicle to exercise perverse and perverting actions towards their children. Such actions are directly related to these women's own experiences of mothering, going back at least three generations. There are few psychoanalytic studies dealing with the particular psychopathol-ogy of perverse relations between mother and child. However, among these, the works of Melitta Sperling (1959, 1963, 1964) are helpful in providing further understanding of the findings I am putting forward. Sperling's observations include childhood ex-periences in the lives of perverse patients, in which the relationship between mother and child is described as a perverse type of object relationship and considered as a crucial factor in the pathological development of both ego and superego functioning of the child.

Nevertheless, it is disappointing that even though Sperling re-fers to a "perverse type of object-relationship", and takes mothers of transvestite boys into analysis prior to taking the children, she never again refers to perverse motherhood. Even when Sperling is advocating the treatment of mothers of perverse attitudes in their motherhood, she refers instead to highly valued maternal func-tions. For my part, I believe that those patients were abusing their position of power as mothers, and that they were exhibiting what I would call perverse maternal attitudes.

In comparing the erotic differences between men and women, Stoller (1991) asserts that men's propensity for fetishizing can in fact be contrasted with the opposite desire in women for relationship, intimacy, and constancy. The problem is that if women fail to obtain these "feminine" qualities in their relationships, they could fall into perverse behaviour. Fantasies of revenge against their partners could then materialize in motherhood using their children as dehumanized, fetishistic objects of which they are in complete control. Stoller himself in his clinical work with male-to-female transsexuals describes how his patients treated him as their mothers had treated them—as an appendage, not as a separate person. He also defines the specific task required from a mother with a growing son in order for him to be acknowledged as a male and to fix the sense of maleness and pride in his own masculinity. This outcome will not be reached when an intense process of symbiosis takes place between mother and infant. Mothers of future transsexuals do not facilitate a process of separation and individuation in their sons. On the contrary, they treat the baby boy as their missing phallus and as the "happy completion of their formerly inadequate body" (Stoller, 1975a, p. 158).

Joyce McDougall (1995) asserts that Winnicott's (1958b) concept of the baby's "capacity to be alone" is easily endangered because of the mother's own anxieties, unconscious fears, and wishes. This makes the baby need to feel like constantly seeking his mother's presence, and according to McDougall, creates an addictive relationship to the mother's physical presence and her caretaking functions. This condition, according to her, is actually created by the mother who is in "a state of dependency with regard to her infant" (1995, pp. 186–187). The infant left unable to identify with a containing figure will appeal, in times of internal turmoil and despair, to addictive objects, which she calls "transitory objects". These, unlike transitional objects, fail in providing a consistent sense of well-being because they utilize somatic attempts rather than psychological ones in dealing with absence. It is particularly relevant in this context to remember this patient's self-referral letter, in which he vividly described not only his psychic pain but also the production of physical symptoms.

I would call his particular predicament a case of "superimposed" transsexualism. In doing so, I am supported by Stoller's assertion that true transsexuals never have episodes of masculinity, whereas my patient had a long-standing happy marriage which had produced four children, adult at the time of his consultation. His wife had telephoned me to let me know that her husband was a *"real man"*, indicating that both were able to enjoy a happy marriage including a fulfilling sexual life. I consider that the reason for his consultation had to do with a mid-life crisis, when he saw himself as an ageing, unattractive man with a receding hairline and bulging waistline; he was in terror of being rejected and left alone because of his physical appearance, just as he had felt when living with his aunt.

We do not have any access to this patient's mother's motivations for sending him away and neglecting him to the point of not visiting him. About his aunt's motivations for bringing him up as a girl, we could speculate that she was trying to replace her dead daughter, perhaps deeply absorbed in pathological mourning. My clinical work has shown me the dangers of a quick "replacement" pregnancy, by which I mean that at times we treat women as if they were factories to produce babies. Many people, including health workers, inappropriately advise bereaved families to proceed in conceiving a new pregnancy. A cherished pet, however, is not usually replaced after death before its owners have had some time to overcome the feelings of grief.

We have learned from Stoller (1968) that one of the very important components in the production of the child's core gender identity is the infant–parent relationship, in particular the psychological aspects of the oedipal and pre-oedipal relationships. The mother's acknowledgement of her child's sex plays an extremely important part in establishing and confirming its core gender identity.

In talking of early infancy, Winnicott (1953a) establishes important differences between the transitional object and the fetish. Whereas the transitional object is part of a normative process and is eventually given up and "relegated to limbo", the fetish dates from infantile experience in the transitional field, and it has the persistence of a specific object or type of object from those early days. In Winnicott's (1953a) terms, the transitional object is used by the pervert to be invented, manipulated, used and abused, ravaged and discarded, cherished and idealized, symbiotically identified with, and de-animated all at once. This is exactly what I believe takes place in the perverse mother's mind and through her manipulation of her baby from which she derives a momentary sense of sexual relief from her increasing sexual tension and anxiety. In other words, the baby becomes for such a mother her transitional object, as proposed by Stoller (1968). Granoff and Perrier (1980) make a similar comment on the type of perverse relationship a mother establishes with her baby in which the baby is first identified as her missing phallus and then becomes her "toy" or "thing"; this they see "as analogous to the part-object relationships of fetishistic perverts" (p. 85, my translation).

Winnicott (1960c) said that babies achieve their true self through good-enough mothering. However, this is more easily said than done, since mothers are also the children of their own mothers with their own range of early ordeals and traumas. My hypothesis, based on my clinical observations, is that mothers who exhibit these perverse tendencies towards their children do so within the first two years of the life of their infants. They are likely themselves to have been the recipient of deficient mothering in their early years, as will have their own mothers before them through at least three generations. Perverse mothers use their babies as transitional objects or actually as fetishes to gain relief from sexual tension and anxiety. Such pathological intimacy is a special form of abuse and has far-reaching transgenerational consequences.

# CHAPTER THREE

# Primary maternal persecution

*Joan Raphael-Leff*

Winnicott backs up his much-quoted aphorism that "there is no such thing as a baby" by quoting Freud's footnote referring to a psychical system of infant and maternal care (Freud, 1911b). In his theory of the parent–infant relationship, Winnicott (1960b) focuses on early emotional development within the psychic system and the impact of maternal care in facilitating or failing a baby's journey from absolute dependence. In this chapter, I examine this mother–infant psychic system from the other point of view—that of the emotional impact on the *woman* of being in close contact with a dependent newborn who has come out of her body and for whom she is responsible. I propose to treat this system as a prenatal rather than postnatal one, and, furthermore, I consider the possibility that within this interactive system, far from experiencing benevolent "primary maternal preoccupation" (Winnicott, 1956a), some mothers may be caught up with what I have termed "primary maternal persecution" (Raphael-Leff, 1986).

Let me here pose an aphorism of my own: "An infant does not begin with conception." The idea of a baby that a woman holds in her mind during pregnancy is not a new one but has been evolving gradually in her psychic reality since her own infancy, nourished by conscious encounters and unconscious residues of all the babies embedded in the transgenerational lineage of reproductive narratives in which she herself is a part (Raphael-Leff, 1996). As Winnicott (1935) said, "Fantasy is part of the individual's effort to deal with inner reality" (p. 130). Imagery of the unborn baby is therefore further complicated by investment of facets of the woman's own baby-self, her aspirations, anxieties, dreams, and desires, as well as positive and negative identifications with both the foetus inside her and with the archaic pregnant mother of her own gestation. The resultant benign, ambivalent, or malevolent fantasy-baby growing alongside the foetus inside her foreshadows and influences the mother's encounter with her newborn. These mental representations of the imaginary baby fade only gradually as unique features of the real child come into focus. I propose that the nature of a mother's concern for her infant will be defined by the degree to which she sees the child as a singular individual, reflecting her capacity to process transferences and to integrate good and bad representations of self and significant others, and to accept her own mixed love and hate reactions to the experience of motherhood.

## The perinatal system

Commenting on the intermediate state between neonatal primary narcissism and interpersonal relationship, Winnicott likens this state to the womb, wherein a set of substances (amniotic sac, placenta, and endometrium) provide essentials until separation occurs (Winnicott, 1988). I suggest that the intrauterine environment not only constitutes an analogy but also sets a precedent for postnatal maternal containment. In addition, I see it not merely as a provisionary situation, but, indeed, as a system, in which the foetus both receives and gives out.

Functionally, the placental system is an active two-way process, redistributing both provisions and pathogens, pumping nutrients and excreting waste products, transmitting toxins, hormones, infections, and imbalances in both directions across the placental barrier. Depending on qualities of the constructed fantasy baby and representation of her own inner resources in the gestating mind of the pregnant woman, different positive or negative aspects of this dyadic system may be emphasized, from bountiful provider of maternal supplies to mutual enrichment by pooled resources, through anxious threats of unidirectional hatred or risk of reciprocal depletion, including exploitation, pollution, or control by foetus and mother. Clearly, antenatally, a persecutory situation may exist if the mother envisages the tethered twosome neither as a blissful symbiotic merger guided by her own benign matronage, nor as a reciprocal coexistence of love and hate, but rather as a parasitic tyranny or as an inescapable experience of mutual damage (Raphael-Leff, 1993, 1995, 1996).

Such an experience of primary maternal persecution may predominate throughout pregnancy. The mother may feel locked into an indissoluble twosome with a malevolent squatter who en-dangers her: "This baby just expels everything bad into me. I'm convinced that's why I'm nauseous—he gets rid of stuff and I absorb it." Alternatively, she may feel herself to be symbiotically engaged with a fragile foetus who is endangered by her: "If I get angry I can feel the baby scrabbling about trying to escape." A mother might also feel both experiences: "When I had the miscarriage, the image in my mind was that I had suffocated the baby—it terrified me that I had to share my resources and allow myself to be sapped. It felt like the interaction with my mother—as if only one of us can thrive, and then always at the expense of the other."

Clearly there is another strand to antenatal persecutory experience—namely, the mother's own internal mother: "I don't want my mother in my pregnancy", said one woman trying to conceive, adding: "She has no boundaries. She created a moat around herself to avoid absorbing me; sadly, it stops me getting close to her but doesn't stop her intruding. She's so intense . . . got interfering, clutching claws. I don't want her to contaminate my insides by poking around—it makes me want to exclude her before I've even started."

## Primary maternal preoccupation

According to Freud (1930a), "Pathology has made us acquainted with a great number of states in which boundary lines between the ego and external world become uncertain or in which they are actually drawn incorrectly" (p. 66). Freud does not mention child-bearing in this context; however, during the normal state of pregnancy, boundaries are crossed in extraordinary ways. Above all, the mother's corporeal world actually incorporates another within her body boundary. Indeed, *two people* reside in her body, foment-ing uncertain distinctions between self and other. In addition, there is a blurring of clear borderlines between outer and inner, between her female body and the male impregnator's contribution to the foetus growing inside her, between conscious fact and un-conscious fantasy, and between past and future babies, mercurial memory and reality to come. It is noteworthy that following expul-sion of the baby with birth, her expanded body-schema subsides only gradually, and, for many a mother, self-boundaries extend at first to include the baby, who during pregnancy has lived inside the confines of her skin. During the period following birth, tempo-rarily, like the neonate, many a new mother seems to lack the limiting membrane differentiating "me" from "not-me", and the mother continues to envelop both self and baby within her orbit. If ever there was a psychic system, surely it is this postnatal dual unit (Mahler, Pine, & Bergman, 1975).

Such a mother may be said to reside in the state that Winnicott (1956a, p. 302) referred to as "primary maternal preoccupation", which he defined as "a very special psychiatric condition of the mother", comparable to a withdrawn or dissociated state or figure during which the parturient is sensitized to meet the infant's body needs. Here, too, system qualities of the interchange are evident. In an exquisitely coordinated progression, a mother is gradually re-leased from this state of immersion in her baby after the early weeks, as her bodily limits gradually contract and her psychic borders are redrawn. Concurrently, the baby begins to take on an identity as a separate human being, as yet unknown, different from herself, yet also similar in having complex human emotions like her own. A leisurely disjunction enables the mother to achieve the *"graduated failure of adaptation"* recommended by Winnicott (1954, p. 203).

By degrees, magical empathy gives way to a more cognitive response to the non-verbal signals, as the mother enters into a dialogue with her increasingly alert baby (Winnicott, 1960b). When mother and infant are well matched, autonomic transmissions *in utero* are replaced by a cascade of interlocking feeding, sleeping, and holding patterns, and an incrementally sophisticated transactional exchange comes into play. Neonatal researchers such as Colwyn Trevarthen (1979), Daniel Stern (1994), and others have established how, under the aegis of the caregiver's attuned responses and respect for the baby's rudimentary communications, an increasingly robust turn-taking proto-conversational exchange develops intuitively between caregiver and infant, the one speaking high-pitched "motherese" and the other emitting finely tuned babble, each vocalization responding yet also eliciting, modulating, and provoking reciprocal replies. This complicated system is founded on mutual expectancies of characteristic interactions, organized through vocal rhythm and through shared states operating across the modalities of time, space, affect, and arousal (Beebe & Lachmann, 1988). However, it is noteworthy that the intricate system of communication between ordinary mothers and babies is far from perfect, with quite a high percentage of misunderstandings, which are subject to continuous repair of ruptures and recovery of attunement (Tronick & Gianino, 1986). Thus, we may say that within a short period of time, the dyadic placental system (physical and emotional) is replaced by a more complex and increasingly verbal system of interdigitating family relationships.

## Primary maternal persecution

However, for many mothers, mental parturition does not constitute a smooth transition. For some, the caesura of birth may shatter the mother–infant conjoined system. Plagued by the sense of loss of an essential part of her self in the process of birth and feeling unable to mend the fractured system, a mother suffering from annihilation of her sense of continuity in the early postnatal days may unconsciously locate the dislocated part of herself in the baby expelled from within her. Postnatal reactions vary depending on the structure of the defences. Often, in this dynamic, a new mother experiences a massive loss of the pregnant state of blooming, feeling full, and seeming greater than the sum of her usual self. Her contraction is exacerbated by social attention now focused on the baby rather than on her pregnant self. As one woman noted: "I can't stand the way he's always surrounded by a circle of adoring relatives, just like my baby brother was." A narcissistic woman may turn the child into an enhancing appendage of the self, which, although inhibiting recognition of the child's authenticity, offers opportunities for exhibitionism and indirect admiration. Invested in the baby are unconscious wishes of rebirth and split-off idealized potentialities of her personality and glorified components of archaic figures to which she is unable to relate consciously but without which she feels incomplete.

However, to others, this externalization results in considerable personal impoverishment, and in borderline disorders the degree of banishment of vital components of the self into the baby may be such that, after the birth, the mother is left feeling empty, depersonalized, and unable to retain a solid sense of self. A woman may imagine herself vanishing, her adult identity and hard-won competence threatened by contact with the wanton baby. Another woman might experience herself as falling apart, decentralized, literally seeing parts of her body as distanced, not belonging to her, fading, or even absent in the mirror. Pseudo-hallucinations, bodily delusions, and a lack of substantiality are not uncommon in states of severe puerperal distress, as the familiar sense of her own being is further undermined by rapid biochemical changes and by the bodily and psychological impact of powerful birth experiences coupled with loss of her pre-pregnant identity and familiar life-style, all this compounded by sleep deprivation, the alienating environment of hospital, and the life and death demands of her new role. In some women, feelings of loss of self, strangeness, anxious foreboding, and de-realization often persist despite the return home, and places, people, objects, and even the baby, too, may appear blurred, unreal, threatening, or bizarre (Raphael-Leff, 1994).

A second kind of persecutory puerperal experience is one not of translocation of self but manifestation of the hidden. The baby represents repudiated aspects of the mother's own baby-self, or intolerable facets of her own internal world. External displacement of this portion of her inner self elsewhere takes place by means of a process of projective identification, which, as Melanie Klein suggested, can serve to rid the self of unwelcome elements by locating it in someone who then can be controlled (Klein, 1946). However, babies ordinarily discredit her façade by parading her secret weaknesses. Although this is a source of great shame, it also allows for vicarious expression of suppressed or prohibited facets of the woman's self. However, as well as disclosure of her infantile faults, unless the child collaborates in decorous behaviour, it poses a constant threat of revealing her maternal shortcomings too, by the simple means of screaming in the supermarket and showing her up in public as a bad mother.

An ironic twist in the closed-system loop is the notion that the exacting infant, who has been inside her and who knows all her defects, is by its very existence experienced as damaged or as accusatory. This private form of persecution particularly affects women with what I call a "maligned self structure", where ordinary needs have been deemed unreasonable or perverse, or where women have suppressed traumatic or abusive events that have not been processed. Anxious or phobic reactions to the baby may arise when every cry or look is interpreted as the baby manifesting damage that she has caused. When paranoid relations prevail, the baby may be seen to be harping on her faults, competing for resources, complaining about the insufficiency of her provisions, criticizing her loving capacities, or, in a self-fulfilling prophecy, provoking her liability to resort to savage retaliation.

Furthermore, a baby opens doors to the past. The caregiver's contact with the baby, intimate in the most primitive sense, is largely mediated through bodily means. We are all familiar with the experience of a certain smell triggering recall of a long-forgotten event. I suggest that in those first weeks of the baby's life, the new mother dealing with primary substances of milk, blood, faeces, urine, vomit, and mucus is bombarded by infantile emotions, which, seemingly, through preconscious sensory memories, propel her back into the sensual world of babyhood, flooding her with reawakened early experience. Winnicott describes the role of maternal holding in facilitating gradual establishment of the infant's psyche within the soma and integration in the face of unthinkable anxieties of going to pieces, falling forever, having no relationship to the body, and having no orientation (Winnicott, 1962). At the point when she is so crucially responsible for sensitive management of her baby's most basic bodily and psychic needs, not only is the mother continuously exposed to the evocative smell, feel, suck, sound, and naked emotions of a tiny infant, oozing primal matter from every orifice, but this puerperal arousal happens at the very time when she herself feels sensitive and regressed, incontinent, leaking, passing lochea and clots, and recovering from the after-effects of birth-pummelling, while suffering from interrupted nights, uterine contractions, and hormonal fluctuations. Close and unmitigated contact with the infant reactivates her own early experiences of feeling helpless, needy, and frustrated. Cata-pulted into a morass of inchoate sensations, strange cravings, and preverbal hurt, inexplicable passions rage within her in bittersweet profusion, at times almost overpowering in their intensity. A new mother who feels painfully aroused and susceptible to unprocessed or distressing emotions with herself may defend against the risk of being overwhelmed by unconsciously ascribing features of her own infantile distress to the newborn, towards whom she then becomes oversolicitous, vicariously trying to heal her own hurt, or from whom she then distances herself in phobic fear of contamination, creating an impermeable barrier within their dyadic system.

In addition to emotional flooding, puerperal disturbance may also take the form of involuntary flashbacks to early trauma. Particularly powerful among these are experiences of repressed infantile events, which are often suddenly retrieved through potent triggers of early motherhood. In these cases, the original primitive emotions, unmodified by time and reality, are released intact in their heightened form, frighteningly unmitigated and unintegrated. I have described these encapsulated emotional phenomena as "geodes", like the solidified bubbles of prehistoric gas that cracked open, hundreds of millions of years after their formation, to reveal their primordial crystalline structure (Raphael-Leff, 1994, p. 27).

## Maternal ambivalence

Winnicott is one of the few psychoanalytic theoreticians who acknowledges maternal ambivalence—the coexistence of hate alongside love, which is inevitable in all live relationships. For those who may ask why a mother is liable to hate her baby, Winnicott lists many reasons, including the baby's ruthlessness, autonomy, oblivion, and interference in her life. In his view, awareness of her own ambivalence enables a woman to "tolerate hating her baby without doing anything about it" (Winnicott, 1949a, p. 74). However, while drawing attention to it, he neglects to comment on the creative role of maternal hatred (cf. Parker, 1994).

Not only does the baby represent a new force in her life, but it represents aspects of the mother's self and inner world, revitalizing old forces, recasting the daughter in the role of her own parent or parents, as well as retriggering her own infantile experiences and fantasied baby-self. I have suggested three powerful precipitants of primary maternal persecution pertaining to self–baby–mother: the sense of loss of an essential part of the self, the baby as manifestation of a hidden part of the self, and exposure to the raw emotions of the baby in her care.

I would like to conclude by linking maternal ambivalence with the two overlapping dyadic systems—her fantasy baby and herself as mother, and herself as fantasied baby with her own archaic mother. I suggest that, especially in the early weeks and months, until a woman can extricate herself from projective identification, we may formulate several different modes of dealing with maternal ambivalence, depending on the prevailing distribution of love and hate in the internal and external systems:

- Idealization      Love [Hate].
- Distancing       Hate [Love].
- Splitting          Love / Hate.

- Conflict          Love versus Hate.
- Ambivalence       Love and Hate.

A mother may wallow in a regressive state of primary identification with her baby, relishing their interchangeability, feeling elated, healed, and regenerated by the bountiful care that she lavishes on the baby and, by proxy, on her own idealized baby-self. In her primary maternal preoccupation, she becomes the glorified mother that she wishes she had had, or she triumphs over the mediocre one that she feels she did have. Fear of ambivalence leads this overfacilitating mother to beatify their contact, denying her own hatred, and suppressing any negative expressions of the baby. However, self-persecution inevitably sets in with extreme guilt at any failure. As one mother expressed it: "How can I ever forgive myself? The baby-alarm was switched off and I didn't hear her crying. She's scarred for life." The resultant overprotectiveness tends to perpetuate their dyadic system beyond its time, while sudden breaks in their fusion may cause seepage of her deep-seated jealousy, morbid anxiety, or angry disillusionment. "We were idyllically happy until her first taste of solid food," said a puzzled breast-feeding mother, noting, "I don't know what got into her but she's a changed baby and has never seemed satisfied since."

In my clinical experience, the converse is true too. When ambivalence is denied, what is suppressed may be not maternal hatred but love. A mother may dread falling in love with her baby, afraid of being sucked into recognition of infantile phenomena in herself, particularly if she regards the baby's needs as weaknesses. To avoid the persecutory experiences described above, she may channel her potential arousal into a regime of regulatory baby-care activity that obviates the need for empathic intuition and identification (Raphael-Leff, 1985, 1986, 1991). Likewise, a woman may go to lengths to avoid indulging or spoiling the baby, out of determination to be the opposite of her own over-loving mother, or out of envy for the baby having the loving mother that she never had. Where love has become dangerous, what is feared unconsciously is the depth of her own loving passion, should it be aroused. A mother may be wary that her pent-up desire could consume the baby or that maternal preoccupation might submerge her identity as a person in her own right. "I will not be the smothering mother mine was", resolves one mother. "I don't want him to become so dependent on me that if I went away he'd miss me", says another. "I dread becoming so involved in baby-care that I lose my brain", says yet another mother. Holding her love in abeyance, and seeking shared care if help is available, she protects both herself and the baby from the presumed dangers of exclusive contact.

When the mother has herself suffered in her infancy from chronic impingements to her own "going-on-being" (Winnicott, 1963a, p. 340), and if indeed her very existence has been negatively defined as persecutory to her own caregivers, she may experience her needs as freakish and her self as wrong. I would like to suggest that in these cases, the self that evolves develops not as a sanitized false self, based on compliance with parental expectations, but as a maligned self, based on internalization of parental ascriptions of being persecutory, monstrous, or dangerous. She hates who she is, denigrates her capacities, and distrusts her needs. As noted, in pregnancy such a woman often fears contaminating the baby or endangering it with her internal badness, and she becomes tormented postnatally by fears of her contemptible presence itself being harmful to the infant. But, likewise, the foetus may pose a risk of poisoning her internal sense, and the live infant can be a psychic threat to mother's sanity, infecting her with its emotions.

One pattern of avoiding ambivalence is the splitting of love and hate, with hateful thoughts seemingly coming from out of the blue, into the mind of a mother who wishes only to love her baby. According to one mother:

"I found myself with a pillow in my hand putting it over the baby's face. And this voice inside me said: 'kill the monster!' I felt so ashamed I could tell nobody about it but then it got worse, all sorts of horrible ideas, too terrible to mention, some of them erotic too. I love my baby but then I doubt myself and say 'how can I love her if I want her dead?' I told my doctor I was depressed and he gave me Prozac but I really wish there was some drug that could wipe these sinful thoughts away."

It was only many weeks into her psychotherapy that this woman could begin to make the connection between these intrusive thoughts and the repressions of her strict Catholic upbringing, and the severe demands of her perfectionist superego. It took longer for her to recognize that the infant is unconsciously identified with both the lovely and the horrid baby she imagined herself to have been and she played out the imagined dilemma of her postnatally depressed mother. When such a woman is aware of her ambivalence and afraid of damage that might ensue if she is alone with her infant, puerperal disturbance has a depressive flavour; safety is secured by ensuring the constant presence of others to mitigate her noxious caregiving and to act as a check on presumed pollution or damage. However, when the split is denied and the mother, isolated in a nuclear family, is offered meagre support networks and few sublimatory outlets, then she may have no safety valve when the hermetically sealed persecutory psychic system erupts.

Other mothers are consciously aware of their hatred but regard anger or even self-assertion as a dangerous, forbidden force that must be curbed at any cost. Love and hate conflict in their minds. One woman expressed this very strongly: "With my toddler, when our worlds collide, I feel he'll get the upper hand and I'll be taken over." This woman's parents still control her life. She continued:

"I love him so and want to be generous but I feel that if I'm not firm nothing will happen—it will all be an immense floppy jelly and we'll be swamped. But at the same time I'm so afraid of my terrible potential for damage I can't bear to say 'no'. Self-hatred wells up when things go wrong, making me feel guilty but also horribly vengeful. If I get cross, I sense the whole family holding their breath, fearfully waiting for me to erupt. Nothing can be straightforward. I want it all to be lovely, but it's as if everything I'm interested in has to be scavenged secretly. It seems impossible to hold everyone's needs in mind all the time and juggle so no one feels left out. I have to silently claw out space for myself and gouge out little handfuls of time. And sometimes it's so much effort to try and get what I want that it's hard to keep my fury under wraps. I get all churned up inside, like I'll implode if I can't replenish myself. So painful . . . like a wordless fear that envelops me and all I want is to get away but I can't escape. The only options left are despair, rage, or—to take my battery out, put my brain in neutral, and carry on mindlessly without thinking."

Persecution may be concentrated around a specific feature: "I get so upset when my babies cry", says a mother who was expected to parent her mother and was never allowed to be sad as a child:

> "It feels like a huge attack coming at me. They seem so vulnerable, and I just want them to be happy, to be a good mother and make everything right ... but I'm so afraid of getting it wrong—such hunger for approval that I give up my own internal barometer. I always believe everything's my fault, and it doesn't get any better with the next baby. I try so hard, I am so nice and helpful to everyone, I keep going, but then suddenly something snaps, and I just run out of steam. . . . Their crying always feels like a criticism—I feel responsible—blamed, guilty, and useless. . . . Once they get older and can talk, I feel I can make a difference. But even then, I still hate it if they seem sad and unresponsive to my help, or don't take me seriously. I feel so insignificant, anonymous."

Most mothers experience their ambivalence quite consciously, as in the case of the mother who stated: "I've got the sweetest baby, but I could have strangled her when she woke me up for the umpteenth time last night." However, even among "ordinary" mothers, where ambivalence prevails, I must stress that mothering can only be as sound as the weakest link in the woman's own mothering chain. Parenting flounders at the point of hypersensitivity when an emotional Achilles' heel is activated as the child reaches the phase or hurt of the parents' own early developmental failures. For some mothers, it is precisely the early postnatal days that are restorative. Persecution sets in at a later stage, when the baby is mobile or verbal or reaches the age of the mother's own traumatic impasse or imagined beastliness. As one mother commented: "It's hideous! My sweet baby has turned into a repellent monster." With others, once the bewildering first six weeks have passed, the so-called "barbaric", "exploitative", or "alien" baby seems increasingly more human and engaging, causing one mother to reflect that "I was terrified by the bundle of instincts until the person in my baby came to life".

In conclusion, parenthood poses inordinate demands of forbearance and can precipitate great distress in those made susceptible by puerperal arousal, collapse of a fragile false self, or increasing insecurity in a maligned self-structure. It is not overstated to say that in many ways, the durable baby who survives maternal difficulties is as encouraging to the carer as is the mother who survives the child's aggression. Successfully negotiating a persecutory phase with one baby can dramatically alter a woman's psychic reality and self-image, lessening her vulnerability with the next baby. One woman noted: "With my first, I felt I had a hole in my thinking process. I cut off from him, and all I could think was that I wanted my mind back. This time I knew it would pass, and that made it so much easier to give myself over to it." This woman had suffered from postnatal depression. However, by the same token, an unmitigated persecutory experience with one baby can lower a woman's tolerance, rigidifying defences and exacerbating her narcissistic, paranoid, or phobic stance as she anticipates with dread a repeat experience with the next child.

## Perinatal therapy

Childbearing in all its phases is a potent reactivator of primal vulnerabilities, unresolved conflict, and unprocessed tensions from the past. Most importantly, a mother is not merely in a solipsistic state of regressive arousal, but is actively involved in engagement with a real infant, and her engagement determines the child's experience. Primary identification with her own infant evokes in a mother a transferential capacity to provoke the very environmental reactions and failures that she herself encountered as an infant. She materializes her past in the present. It is important to make a distinction between *depressive experiences*, which are tormenting because the woman feels herself to be innately damaged and insufficient or potentially destructive, and *persecutory experiences*, where a mother feels threatened by a bloodthirsty infant representing an internal figure or some split-off aspect of her baby self, or by an injurious situation or mutually harmful relationship. One avenue of bringing traumata under the jurisdiction of her omnipotent control is to use her power to inflict impingements on her infant or to induce the baby to inflict them on her. Another is the use of excessive gratification of the baby, to attempt to compensate herself for original deprivations or to ensure that the baby rewards her.

Individual psychotherapy or mother–infant psychotherapy can provide a thinking space for the woman who has been thrust back into the emotional turbulence of her childhood persecution. By gathering catastrophic reawakenings and persecutory anxieties into the safety of the therapeutic sphere, a hierarchy of holding is established, providing a model of thinking about feelings, enabling the mother thus held by the processing psychotherapist to contemplate rather than act and, by understanding and accepting her own infantile needs, to recognize the reality of her child rather than magically realizing projections transferred from her past. Perinatal therapy, during pregnancy or the postnatal period, offers the woman an opportunity to repossess her own early suffering rather than bypassing it by providing an idyll, tyrannically passing it on, splitting, denying, or enacting it—all forms of vicarious exploitation of the transference-child held in her body or in her arms. Through self-reflection within the transitional space of psychotherapy, the transgenerational chain of persecution can be broken.

# CHAPTER FOUR

# Children who kill their teddy bears

*Valerie Sinason*

"And they smiled so sweetly
as they ate her dolls and bears
she knew no toy could hold her"

Valerie Sinason, "The Re Naming", 1982

In 1903, Rainer Maria Rilke, anticipating Donald Winnicott's (1953a) paper on transitional objects by nearly fifty years, understood many of the emotional uses to which a toy, a "thing", could be put in the service of the child's developmental needs. In being the first not-me possession, it must survive loving and hating; it can be cuddled, attacked, and mutilated; it has to appear to have some life of its own, to not be an hallucination; it must be able to contain in its actuality the longings, needs, and projections of the child; and finally, it is neither forgotten nor mourned, but eventually loses meanings. It stands for the first relationship, largely that with the mother.

With loving, good-enough parenthood, the child can negotiate the ordinary painful difficulties of life and achieve the disillusionment that comes from having been allowed the state of illusion previously. The child can move from magical control to muscular control, and finally let go. The thumb, the corner of the blanket, the teddy bear, the doll, can all finally be put aside but not disappear. At times of adult difficulty, they can return as cigarettes, as drink, as executive toys, or even as transitional people. Where there are greater difficulties, they are transformed into fetishes where they continue their life in various forms of adult sexuality.

However, in childhood, what happens when the child has received terrible experiences? What has happened when a child tries to "kill" its transitional object? I focus here on physically and sexually abused latency-age children who were also severely learning disabled. All of these children were well known in their different settings for attacks on what one boy called his "deaded" teddy bears. Within the psychotherapy room, all the children repeated this behaviour.

## CASE ONE: STEVEN

"Steven" was 8 years old. He was mute, brain-damaged, and severely disabled. He was covered in bruises, infected cuts, and dirt, and he was dressed in clothes that were far too small for him. He behaved as if he knew that he was dispensable. At home he ran into roads, fell off bikes, and got knocked over by cars. Abuse had been proven but not who had committed it. Steven did not, would not, or could not communicate such information. Social Services were convinced that both parents were sexually and physically abusing him, but his muteness, severe disability, and "accident-proneness" had somehow led to their reluctance to remove him, despite his mother's regular statement that she should have "cut him out" before her pregnancy had advanced. Her death wishes towards Steven were regularly expressed verbally.

In Steven's first session, after months of muteness, he stared at me, with great difficulty opened his mouth, moved his lips soundlessly, and then with great force, with his fists clenched, uttered the single word "kill". The novelist William Golding (1980) could have been writing about Steven when he said, "Not only did he clench his fists with the effort of speaking, he squinted. It seemed that a word was an object, a material object, round and smooth sometimes, a golf-ball of a thing that he could just about manage to get through his mouth, though it deformed his face in the passage" (p. 19). Shortly after, Steven picked up a musical toy that I had in the room. This toy provided the opportunity of making different sounds, bells, whistles, drums. I always provide musical toys for mute (electively or organically) and learning-disabled children and adults (Sinason, 1988b, 1992). He bashed it. Then he tried to blow its whistle. I said that he wanted to see if it still had a voice after it was hurt.

Steven put the toy in the sink and poured water over it. He said that the water was ice-cold. Then he tried desperately to whistle through it again. I said that perhaps it was a voice box like his and that he was seeing how much he could do before the voice died. He nodded sadly and said, "It goes to heaven. Then it flies. It is a ghost, a dead voice." A little while later, he leaped onto the window sill, calling, "I don't really think you want to kill me, mummy". I caught him up and carried him down, saying that he was offering to hurt himself first to stop me hurting him, because I seemed such a dangerous and bad mother. He agreed. Then Steven went to the teddy bear in his box, and with a sharp pencil he poked through its voice box. "Kill, kill, kill", he repeated, with terrible power coming from his voice. "Stupid little baby teddy!", he shouted, ranting, "You can't talk! You can't speak! I have stopped you!" He then went to the dressing-up cupboard and put on an apron. "I'm my mummy", he said to me. He returned to the teddy and picked up the pencil like an offensive weapon. Steven asked, "Cat got your tongue? I'm the cat. Stupid baby! Cry baby! You can't talk! Kill!"

Each week, Steven would return to the increasingly mutilated teddy and the musical toy—these were the only toys that counted. They carried his psychic death inside themselves, and for that they were objects of love and terror. Steven asked, "Why aren't you deaded? I kill you enough times". Steven had learned that transitional phenomena cannot be killed. The undead teddy and the ghost of the voice, the voice in its coffin, were becoming a persecution, as would be known to all who make horror films.

The terrible word "kill" that hurt his face coming out, the terrible birth that had damaged the fantasied body of his mother, turned out, in fact, to be the embodiment of his mother's death-wish towards him. It was not the baby Steven who destroyed his mother by being born. However, the unwanted child, as the child of an unwanted child, became the receptacle for dis-owned hatred. Rascovsky and Rascovsky (1968) have com-mented that our professional neglect over cruel parenting is due to universal resistance to acknowledging the filicidal drives of the mother herself.

*CASE TWO: JOHNNY*

Then there was "Johnny", aged 8 years, tiny, thin, and on the child protection register for failure to thrive. He was mildly learning-disabled, and he would sit for hours in trance-like stages, moving his hands or feet in strange patterns. He would come out of these states either desperately offering himself for sexual attention, presenting his buttocks to the older boys, or thrusting his pelvis, or he could suddenly throw himself into violent action with no apparent warning. Every week, Johnny came for psychotherapy calling out, "Give me blood", in an ogre-like voice. I wondered to myself what horror film he might have been watching. However, after eight months, I be-came suddenly aware that I was not properly thinking about Johnny's words. They worried me so much that I had turned them into nasty videos in order to distance myself from them.

On one particular day, one year into the psychotherapy, Johnny strode up and down the treatment-room saying in his usual way, "Give me blood. Give me blood". I made the comment, "Somebody seems to need a lot of blood today". Johnny went white, shook, and hid under the table, clutching his dirty Rupert Bear. "How did you know?", he asked, terrified. I was still myself shaken by the sight of his terror, by the pallor on his face, by his dilated pupils, and by the tight grip with which he held onto Rupert. It took me a while to say that there was something that I had not known for a long time, but today I seemed to know some things better.

"I am going back now. I am a ghost", he said. Children often pretend to be ghosts, sometimes acting out bereavement fears and fantasies, sometimes replaying a television programme. However, there was something different here, and my response was different. "How did you get to be a ghost?", I asked. Johnny replied, "Well, it's better being a ghost because if you are dead, they can't hurt you any more". I felt enormously sad. "Poor ghost", I said, noting that, "then it is a good job you can find a way of surviving". "Yes", he said, suddenly more restored, saying to me, "And now I am going back to hell". "Right", I said, "That must be a difficult place to get to. How do you get there?" "By the trap-door next to the cooker in my kitchen", he replied. A chill entered the room and into myself.

A week later, taking a sharp pencil and scissors, Johnny drew an occult shape on the teddy bear. Then, with surgical precision, he pulled off the outer skin and pulled out the pieces of stuffing. In my countertransference, I felt nausea (Sinason, 1988a). He picked up a toy plate, and then he filled a beaker with water; then he poured water over some of the stuffing. Johnny explained: "This is blood spaghetti. It's from my teddy. I have to eat it or they'll kill me."

I said that must be very hard having to eat the inside of his teddy. "Easier than my dog", he said. He then let out a piercing shriek. "I'm mad. Everything I say is mad", he screamed. He put red paint onto the stuffing from the teddy. "Dead dog, eat the dead dog. Dead teddy. You have to eat it all or you will be in trouble. Come and eat!", he cried. He turned towards me. "Come on! Mummy and Daddy have got lovely food ready for you. Dead dog. Lovely dog steaks, dog spaghetti, lovely blood drink. Come back from school children and enjoy your food", he uttered.

Perhaps it was only then that I was able to see that Rupert Bear was a particularly dirty colour because almost daily Johnny would bury him under the earth in the back garden, once even making a cardboard coffin. However, like Steven, he had come to realize that this thing, this experience, this feeling projected into the toy, could not be buried. Rupert Bear was undead, unburied. I have written elsewhere (Hale & Sinason, 1994; Sinason & Svensson, 1994) of the plight of adult survivors of satanist abuse. Many have told me that their abusing parents, themselves abused as children, encouraged them to love a toy or a pet, only in order to exert their power by making the child kill it or eat it. Betrayal and dismemberment is the order of the day, generationally transmitted.

## CASE THREE: THE CHILDREN'S GROUP

"Adam" undressed the baby dolls and made them have intercourse. He said that there was a babysitter, but she had left, and that the house had caught on fire. He asked me to call the fire brigade. I did that, and he then became a fireman, passing the dolls to me. Adam said that one baby had died. He covered its head, and then he said that I was the mother and that I could kiss it goodbye. I noted that I was perhaps a bad mother to leave babies with a no-good babysitter. He said that the other babies might have to go into care, and I agreed, saying that if I could not look after them properly no matter how much I love them, then they did have to go into care. There was a painful silence.

"Beatrice" tried to stir Adam back to his previous behaviour, chanting, "Go on—fuck the baby dolls—kick the teddy's balls—smash his face in". "Charlie" bashed the teddy, and the others formed a chorus, calling, "Stupid dumb handicapped thing. Don't know your alphabet. Don't know how to read and write. Stupid shit cunt. Pig." Beatrice then got louder, intoning, "My friend Spike can kill people. Go on, Charlie, Adam, kill the fucking ted."

Charlie and Adam looked worried. I said that they did not want to turn into Spike. Charlie looked thoughtful for a moment, then worried, and then he giggled and started bashing the teddy's head into the sink. Then both boys piled abuse and blows onto the teddy. At one point, when both boys collapsed from the exhaustion of the impossible task, Beatrice screamed,

"The fucking thing is dead—you can do what you like". There was a pause, and Diana said, "You all love him—you love that teddy". There was an electric silence, and then they agreed. I found myself reciting silently the final stanza of Oscar Wilde's haunting "Ballad of Reading Gaol": "And all men kill the thing they love / By all let this be heard, / Some do it with a bitter look / The brave man with a sword!"

## Discussion

Like Johnny and Steven, Beatrice knew that if you were dead you could not be hurt. But like all these children, the ghosts from the nursery that they carried could not die (cf. Fraiberg, Adelson, & Shapiro, 1975). They had not been answered and were doomed to haunt. The tragic family relationships that had been damaged for several generations were too powerful to undo. As Selma Fraiberg and her colleagues have noted, "the baby has become a silent partner in a family tragedy", and "That baby in these families is burdened by the oppressive past of his parents from the moment he enters the world. The parent, it seems, is condemned to repeat the tragedy of his childhood with his own baby in terrible and exacting detail" (p. 388).

# CHAPTER FIVE

# Deprivation and delinquency in the treatment of the adolescent forensic patient

## *Jeannie Milligan*

Winnicott (1968) saw delinquency as a sign of hope, because it is essentially object-related. He compared it with the infant's milk-seeking behaviour, whereby a fundamental need may be satisfactorily met by the provision of external resources. He viewed the origins of delinquency as rooted in a sense of deprivation. By this he meant that the infant, having discovered that the desired supplies exist and are accessible, develops the sense of possessing them. However, if the infant then perceives the supplies as disappearing, it suffers the traumatic experience of the loss of a right. Winnicott argued that what underpins the delinquent act is the wish of the infant self to repossess that to which we believed we had a right. The essential characteristic of a delinquent act is that it affects some other person or thing, and it is this quality that allows the possibility of a response. Winnicott argued that it is this active direction in delinquent behaviour that may be understood as the deprived infant-self displacing the search for its rightful possession onto other resources, which may be appropriated by theft. In this way, hopelessness and despair can be avoided. If the delinquent's search can be correctly identified, it may become acceptable for the taking-in of a good substitute for the painfully lost previous response. Winnicott suggested this may take the form of an emotional relationship, or may come about by management of the delinquent's environment.

Psychotherapy offers the space for these issues to emerge, often via being re-enacted in the transference and countertransference, so that ultimately the underlying deprivation may be understood and worked through. Success depends on the extent to which a depressive position, rather than a paranoid–schizoid one, can be more securely and consistently occupied. There are then opportunities to miss and therefore to mourn the object, allowing the possibility of the acceptance of another object, with all its differentness and limitations, to take its place.

I wish to focus on the aspects of this process that are particular to the delinquent adolescent and the adults they encounter in response to their difficult, antisocial behaviour. Additionally, by reference to case material, I want to raise the question of what kind of object the psychotherapist needs to be for a delinquent adolescent patient as opposed to an adult one. I think that the psychotherapist needs to be available for an ambivalence of a particular kind with respect to the characteristics of the adolescent process. On the disturbingly rocky road between childhood and adulthood, the adolescent has to endure massively contradictory feelings at times; some are the reworkings of infantile conflicts and some are new developments resulting from the alarming and uncontrollable changes of the body during puberty. Feeling at odds with one's body, one's parents, one's peers, and perhaps with the world in general is a turbulent experience. Anyone trying to work alongside an adolescent will be challenged in particular ways. For example, there is a pronounced need for consistency in the psychotherapist to withstand infantile omnipotence. Also required is a particular sensitivity to the danger of humiliation in the adolescent, since real helplessness has only recently been experienced in childhood. The therapist needs to offer the experience of Winnicott's good-enough mother who is firm yet flexible, and non-intrusive in the context of the adolescent's highly charged sensitivity to all boundaries but especially those pertaining to the body. The therapist needs to expect a higher-than-usual tendency to act out because of the typical difficulty in the adolescent phase of development of conceptualizing and putting into words states of mind that are difficult, confusing, or painful. That which cannot be borne psychically and symbolized is instead expressed in action. The adolescent who acts out delinquently will inevitably at times relate to his or her therapy in the same way. What is crucial is whether the adolescent's re-enactment in the transference is creative and on the side of development, or perverse and destructively anti-developmental. This fundamentally affects the psychotherapist's ability to preserve a space for thinking, so that we do not just become the recipient of projection, but remain as workers who can hold boundaries appropriately.

Winnicott was under no illusion about the difficulties in such work; however, he believed that a hopeful act may in time be experienced as a previously neglected painful conflict about an abandonment at last being met with the required response. In other words, his contention was that the theatre of negotiation is one of the potential to recover from deprivation, via the experience of being contained in a holding environment. Winnicott's candid assessment of the difficulties of adolescence, combined with his belief that there were interventions that could be both pragmatic and helpful to the adolescent, must have influenced and supported many adults, both professionals and family members, who felt confounded by a situation presented by a delinquent adolescent.

My first such professional encounter occurred during my very first week as a field social worker.

I was asked to prepare a report for the juvenile court on "Sammy", a small 10-year-old boy with an endearing smile, who had just set fire to his primary school, causing thousands of pounds worth of damage. The school staff and the local community were shocked by the magnitude of the act, and by the discrepancy between such destructive violence and the charming imp they had considered Sammy to be. Neither he nor any member of his family had ever been in trouble with the police before. Indeed, they were considered to be a quiet unremarkable family about whom little was known. This case represents my baptism into forensic work with adolescents.

I arranged to visit the home, and I found the family on the edge of chaos. The house had few possessions but was spotlessly clean and tidy. Passing the kitchen on arrival, I noticed that it was starkly bare, with no sign of food. Sammy was the youngest of five children born roughly eighteen months apart. The children greeted me with shy warmth and politeness, then seemed listless and worried, hanging around me in a way that felt to me unusual. Sammy's father made great efforts to welcome me, and alternately smiled with apparent relief that I had come or became distracted, speaking of his anxieties about what to do with the family. I learned that he and his wife had come over to this country as immigrants some eighteen years previously, but the rest of their respective families had remained in their country of origin. All the children had been born in this country. Although the family had never had much money, life had gone quite well until recently. I wondered what had gone wrong.

Sammy's mother then appeared, a strange, wild-looking lady who was extremely suspicious of me and quite out of touch with the reasons for my visit. The father and all the children immediately became subdued and wary, as if in the presence of a time bomb. Sammy himself shrank into his chair and turned his face to the window, staring blankly. During my many subsequent meetings with Sammy and his family, it became clear that his mother had been becoming increasingly mentally ill for some time. On reflection, the father thought that this had begun when she had become profoundly depressed on returning to this country from a visit home to her mother four years previously. He thought that she had deteriorated further as the children had grown up and become busy with their own lives, friends, and school. A gentle, demonstrably affectionate man, Sammy's father obviously cared a great deal for his children and for his wife. He had, effectively, taken on the maternal functions for the parental couple in recent years, since it had become impossible for his wife to undertake them. He was just about managing to juggle a physically demanding job in a bakery, working in the early hours of the morning, with household and parenting tasks. He was at his wits' end, with no friends or family to help. His wife's state of mind had been responded to by the husband and children taking turns to supervise her during the day. This linked with reports from the children's schools that while they were not considered problematic, there was concern about absences and underachieving.

My hypothesis was that Sammy's mother had been able to function as a caring mother when he was little, evidenced by the success of all the children negotiating developmental steps appropriately. However, the very fact that they could develop autonomy left her feeling isolated and abandoned, so that her last visit home confronted her with the pain of separation from her own mother, which had never been worked through. Her withdrawal into increasingly bizarre self-preoccupation would equally have been experienced by Sammy as a traumatic loss of the good-enough mother he had previously had. He was due to leave his primary school, where he had felt safe and at home, to tackle all the demands of secondary school and adolescence. He could not articulate his feelings in words and, instead, drew attention to his plight in the arson attack. The intensity of his sense of deprivation and confusion had become overwhelming, and he no longer had available defences. The raging fire expressed his raging anger which he had been unable to direct towards either of his parents for fear of annihilating them, leaving himself no hope at all of securing the help he needed. The conflict between Sammy's libidinal and aggressive impulses had become intolerable when his exhausted father latterly became unable to sustain his efforts to provide maternal care. Winnicott always emphasized the importance of the external environment in relation to the internal world, referring to its giving a new opportunity for ego-relatedness, and he bemoaned the fact that "over and over again one sees the moment of hope wasted, or withered, because of mismanagement or intolerance" (Winnicott, 1956b, p. 309). He championed the cause of offering management in the environment as an appropriate response, calling it "a going to meet and match the moment of hope" (p. 309). Neither parent could meet Sammy's needs, and so he began to act out, outside the confines of the family; and thus, although he was upset, Sammy could make some sense of the authorities' reactions to his behaviour—for example, his being suspended from school and having to appear in court. In time, he no longer felt under pressure to smile endlessly and to charm, and he could instead be more openly difficult.

Sammy was not, at that point, considered suitable for psychotherapy; instead, aspects of his environment were attended to. I arranged to meet with his father on a weekly basis to offer social-work support for reclamation of stability and a more ordinary life at home. He used the case-work relationship well to attend to his own emotional needs in pursuing the difficult tasks that he so wanted but had previously been unable to pursue. A family aide was provided by Social Services to enable domestic life to get back on the rails. The community psychiatrist made an urgent domiciliary visit to Sammy's mother, psychotropic medication was prescribed, and regular supervision by the community psychiatric nurse was arranged. My request for several adjournments in the court proceedings allowed sufficient time to pass for matters to have improved considerably by the time that a care order was made, so that it was agreed that Sammy should remain placed at home. However, if things were to deteriorate again, Social Services had the authority to place him rapidly into a more holding environment away from his family. At the subsequent case conference, the school agreed to allow Sammy back so that he could finish his primary education properly and have the experience of working through the separation entailed in his moving on to secondary school. In the following two years, with the continued input of psychiatric, education, and social services, things improved a great deal. By then, Sammy's older siblings were leaving school and were successfully starting jobs, and he himself had settled and was doing well at his secondary school. His parents were operating as a working couple again, and they were responding to the children's negotiation of adolescence in a more or less appropriate way.

Winnicott (1963e) frequently linked adolescence with infancy in terms of the individual struggle to find a true self. It is this that gives rise to the delinquent's sense of relief about being caught in the act, when met by a strong parental authority figure. However, such confrontation needs to be of a particular quality in order to be experienced as containing and as non-retaliatory, without vindictiveness, having its own strength. This holds true for the delinquent adolescent in his or her external and internal world. Psychologically, these adolescents are again under pressure from primitive phantasies last encountered directly in infancy. The consequent sense of disturbance is exacerbated by the recognition that they now have the real physical capacity to overpower or to destroy. This combination means that their use of projective identificatory mechanisms is highly charged in particular ways. The manifestation of all this in the psychotherapy relationship of course colours the types of transference and countertransference which emerge during the treatment. "Harry", a 19-year-old boy I saw in once-weekly psychotherapy for two and a half years, focused my thinking on the mixture of difficult problems with valuable opportunities that the psychotherapist is likely to encounter in work with delinquent adolescents.

Because adolescence involves so much reworking of fundamental separation–individuation and oedipal issues, it constitutes a "last-chance" opportunity for development to be enhanced before defensive mechanisms become more broadly spread and rigid. Nevertheless, there is still great pressure to repeat behaviour previously experienced as bringing relief from unbearable tension. To the extent to which this has become compulsive, it will be increasingly difficult to give up in favour of less split-off ways of relating, because excitement and power have become valued secondary gains. The conflict between a genuine wish to move successfully into adulthood and a contradictory attachment to reliable defences (particularly violence and sexualization) was central to Harry's difficulties. As his therapist, I had to try to find ways of negotiating re-enactment of this in the session.

Harry grew up in a prosperous middle-class family, his parents having started their own business when he was 5 years old. He had three older siblings, one of whom had previously had an eating disorder, and another who had had an illegitimate baby when very young. They had all now left home. There was also a fifth, much older half-sibling, born illegitimately to the mother when in her late teens and immediately adopted. This had apparently been kept secret in the family for many years. Harry referred himself for treatment, which I later understood (because the parents themselves undertook a brief period of therapy as a couple in the clinic) in terms of his parents being totally preoccupied with their business. Additionally there were evident marital difficulties, mother being depressed and father being an alcoholic. It was as if they had not registered the extent of Harry's suffering nor his difficulty in leaving home and developing an independent life. It seemed that the whole family had operated an extended system of denial for many years, despite serious emotional problems evidenced by almost all of them. It was encouraging that Harry appeared to have sufficient ego strength to seek out for himself the care and attention that he needed. In his assessment interviews with me, he spoke of persistent suicidal wishes, of feeling paranoid in relation to peers and to the world in general, of a wish to blame everyone else for his plight yet knowing that this was not accurate, and of extreme anxiety about his destructiveness. He observed himself apparently seeking close relationships but then ensuring that they were sabotaged by his cruel attacks. This sadism was not only psychological; he had a history of violent attacks against both his father and his mother. These had never been reported either to the police or to the family doctor, who was a local friend. He had begun to feel that his parents would never take proper notice of his behaviour or of his disturbed state of mind. However, someone else finally had.

Harry had made two attempts to have a girlfriend. He could not account for becoming involved with the first, except that she was sexually available. He remembered how provoked he used to become when she would, as he perceived it, flaunt herself in front of her stepfather's male friends. On one occasion, she apparently asked him to rape her which he quickly began to do, only stopping to think when she started crying. They broke up after this. The second woman was one of his teachers at the design college he attended, fifteen years Harry's senior. He thought that her interest in him was because she was lonely and enjoyed their "deep conversations" as much as he did. He felt that their sexual relationship had been good, but he then remembered an occasion in the recent past when he had felt troubled without knowing quite why. His recollection was that after intercourse she had referred to the semen he had produced and had said "it's not much". Until he started therapy, he had made no connection between this episode and what happened shortly afterwards. He told me how, because it was Valentine's Day, he had sent the woman a "joke letter", anonymously. It described the writer as a stranger who had been secretly following her home from work and, from a hiding place opposite, had been watching her in her house. Explicit details were given of the writer's perverse sexual fantasies about her, and particularly the wish to rape her anally. Harry had no idea why he had written such a letter, and he was surprised by the woman's horrified reaction. She guessed that he was the writer, and though she immediately ended the relationship, she suggested that he sought help; she gave him the address of the clinic where I work. Telling me this in an early session, Harry said that he now felt this was caring of her, and then he said that what he really wanted was for her to hold him while he cried. He said that he was very puzzled by recognizing that he wanted to be comforted like a child, which appeared to have no connection with the excitement in speaking about anal rape.

In the transference, I think I was initially a caring, concerned parental authority figure whom he could not find at home. However, Harry's account led to the likelihood that that position would be under threat of perversion in Harry's mind. Confusion between infantile longings for a good-enough mother with its corruption by *eroticization* became the central *feel* for treatment. Nonetheless, this young person had the capacity to present himself for treatment, and the wish to do so, where he could and did receive psychotherapeutic help.

* * *

I have attempted to provide a glimpse into both the internal mind and the external reality of two adolescent forensic patients. Their histories reveal, exactly as Donald Winnicott had predicted, a great amount of deprivation of parental care, which in all likelihood contributes to the development of delinquent acts. And yet, as Winnicott has noted, one can be hopeful in working with delinquents who do possess the ability to steal what they lack, thus attempting to fill in the emptiness from which they struggle. Once such patients begin to internalize their missing environmental provisions, then the need for acting-out will indeed diminish.

# CHAPTER SIX

# On pseudo-normality:
# a contribution to
# the psychopathology of adolescence

*Donald Campbell*

Over the years I have been struck by the way children and especially adolescents seek reassurance for their anxieties about lagging behind their peers, or feeling strange and abnormal, by trying to achieve what they consider to be a developmental milestone, such as having a girlfriend, passing an important set of exams, or going off to university. The appeal of the achievement of a developmental milestone for the child or adolescent is that it provides a sense that they must be normal after all, because they have been able to do something that is expected of them and, in some cases, that their peers have already accomplished. Parents, teachers, and peers tend to support the fantasy that normality is defined exclusively by the achievement of developmental milestones.

I have found this a very powerful resistance in treatment with adolescents who use their work towards these milestones to avoid the more painful and disturbing regressive pulls in analysis with accompanying passive and infantile longings. I often find it difficult to resist my own wishes for them to progress and, more important, to be seen to be improving. The resistance may also manifest itself as an unspoken termination date which is in the adolescent's mind from the beginning of his or her analysis—a termination date that coincides with the achievement of their developmental milestone (Novick, 1976).

These resistances contribute to a pseudo-analysis, and they are closely related to false-self phenomena, which Winnicott elaborated in his paper "Ego Distortion in Terms of True and False Self" (1960c). These adolescents will make use of the analysis only when it can be seen to further their conscious aim of achieving the milestone within these narrow, goal-orientated parameters. This search for an external solution as a defence against internal development also features in the resistance of adult patients who try to hijack the analysis for the purpose of acquiring a formula for life or for the solution to a particular problem. However, this "hidden agenda" may be easier to see in children and adolescents because it is so directly linked to developmental progress and exposes the precursors to the adult's defensive use of normality.

## The development of a sense of "normal"

*Webster's Dictionary* defines "normal" as "conforming to rules, regular, average, or ordinary". I want to identify in a very condensed fashion particular aspects of the way in which a child develops a sense of what is normal, in order to consider some of the vicissitudes of this process that may contribute to psychopathology. Stern's (1985) review and interpretation of current research in child development identifies the growth of the sense of self as primarily an inter-subjective process. Braten (1987) maintains that the prerequisite for inter-subjectivity is the inherently *dyadic* organization of the individual. Braten has proposed that there are circuits within the newborn's central nervous system that specify the immediate co-presence of a complementary participant, which he refers to as a "virtual other", whose potential is fulfilled by an actual other. The virtual other is a "felt prospective" waiting to be realized by an actual other. The infant and mother thereby create the first dialogic circle by virtue of the mother becoming the first actual other in the infant's life.

Various research workers have elucidated the infant's capacity to cue a response from the parent from as early as 2 months of age, which suggests that the infant has the ability to attract or to stimulate into life the object it is seeking. This object, in turn, becomes the object who will nurture the infant's subsequent development (cf. Brazelton, Koslowski, & Main, 1974; Murray, 1991; Stern, 1974; Trevarthen, 1979). I try in this chapter to demonstrate that a feature of the underlying dynamic between the analyst and the patient is the presence of a virtual other that becomes realized by the actual other as the analyst in the transference. The patient elicits or provokes, grants space, and internalizes the actual other in the analytic relationship.

Observations of infant–mother interactions also illuminate a process in which the child scans the mother and the environment in order to identify experience that either confirms or contradicts its expectations of itself and its universe. Specific memories that result from the mother–infant interaction and share a common denominator become organized together to identify an average expectable experience. In turn, these "islands of consistency" create "expectations of feelings, of sensations, and so on that can either be met or be violated" (Stern, 1985, p. 97). As development proceeds, the child identifies and knits together "islands of consistency" in order to establish a sense of the self based on those aspects of itself that are shareable.

Meaning, in the sense of linking thought and language, results from the same process of interpersonal negotiations between self and object, by what can be agreed upon as shared (Stern, 1985; cf. Vygotsky, 1962). Winnicott (1953a) had already conceptualized this process when he described words as transitional phenomena that occupy space somewhere between the infant's subjectivity and the mother's objectivity. Vygotsky (1962) referred to these mutually negotiated meanings as "we meanings" which develop originally in the interaction between mother and child, but which undergo change later in development as the child interacts with peers. Stern has reminded us that much of the task of psychoanalysis lies in bringing together meaning that is experienced as isolated within the self, or as located entirely somewhere else, in order to rediscover "we meanings".

I have outlined in broad and superficial terms an inter-subjective view of development in order to identify a model for the development of a sense of self that persists in various forms throughout development. With this model in mind, one can see how the child very quickly learns which aspects of its own template, its own constitutional make-up, and its own experiences are shareable and, consequently, become reinforced and established. Thus, that which is shareable becomes the norm. I am suggesting that this is the basic process by which a child develops a sense of normality and, at the most rudimentary level, develops psychic structures and reinforces certain affects, behaviours, and ways of thinking about itself that conform to the norm.

Freud reminded us that the essence of what is normal, and indeed abnormal, arises from within the family and is based on what is or is not accepted by the family. That which is not shareable is quickly experienced as outside the norm, and therefore abnormal, and initially fails to thrive or develop; later, it may create conflicts requiring defensive activity, symptom formation, or distortion of character. However, that which may be normative within the family may be pathogenic outside the family if it deviates from the wider cultural norms.

McDougall (1980) has maintained that within psychoanalytic theory the normative is "defined in terms of the concept of an 'oedipal organisation' within each individual, a *normalizing structure* in the sense that it pre-exists the birth of the child and is destined to structure psychically the child's future intra- and interpersonal relations" (p. 468). If McDougall is right, then the organization of the newborn is inherently triadic, involving three people. The normalizing structure—the oedipal organization—would contain a second, paternal "virtual other" which would become realized by an actual father's response to his child. Failure to realize the virtual other in the child results in a pseudo-normality that remains superficial, external, and unconnected to the felt prospective of the virtual other of the individual's internal world. McDougall draws attention to those patients who have resolved the unacceptable oedipal situation by "conforming to the rules", "fitting into the norm", and being "regular guys". Initially, these individuals appear to be well-adjusted, but upon closer scrutiny it emerges that normality is a *symptom* in that these people function with an unshakeable system of preconceived ideas that prevent any further thought and give the ego-structure the force of a programmed robot. That was my initial impression of "Jason".

*Background*

Jason was 17 years of age when his stepmother called me complaining that she and his father were at the end of their tether with Jason. She claimed that he was conspiring to destroy the family. If something did not change, Jason would have to leave the family.

When I saw Jason for an assessment interview, I was struck by his large, soft, overweight body. He reminded me of an overfed baby. Jason was socially assured, with a warm smile and a "take-charge" approach to the interview. I had the impression that he felt more comfortable with adults than with peers. He was doing well academically, but he had few friends and spent most of his time at home watching television, or lost in daydreams.

When Jason was 6 years old, nine months after the birth of his brother "Stephen", his mother developed breast cancer, and she had a radical mastectomy. The mother developed secondaries within a year, and she was nursed at home until she died a year later. According to his father and his stepmother, Jason, aged 8, coped by writing father a letter empathizing with father's loss and hoping that he would find another wife soon. Two years after the mother died, his father remarried. Jason's stepmother gave birth to a baby girl a year later. Jason was bullied and babyish at school. He regularly sucked his thumb, especially when there was a row in the family. Jason was unable to go to sleep without sucking his thumb.

Initially, Jason wanted me to believe that everything was fine, and that he had a number of formulas for ensuring peace in the family. For instance, he would often say, "If I give, they'll give. If I act adult, I'll be treated like one. Mother didn't bring me here today, I said I could get here myself."

Eventually, Jason told me that from the age of 6 onwards, when his brother Stephen was born, he had felt lost. Since his mother's death, he had remembered only useless things about her, "like the way she dialled the telephone with her middle finger". Here he jumped to what he wanted to be when he grew up: an accountant computing losses and profits. He seemed to get carried away with this, and he brushed aside my link from his interest in losses and profits to his struggle to cope with losing his mother and gaining a stepmother.

Jason also told me that he only thinks of himself as 4 years old or as 24 years old. As a 24-year-old, he imagines himself teaching and living in a flat. He drew floor plans of the flats he intended to live in. He kept looking for someone to be like or to imitate when he became confused about being 17 with a 17-year-old body. Jason said that he could not talk to his father—it was hopeless. His father made lists of acceptable interests that he wanted Jason to develop. Father's lists never included Jason's interests in pop music. He started stealing money from his father to buy sweets for children at school in order to win their friendship. Having sweets like other kids made him feel normal. Jason is closer to his stepmother, but he finds her bossy, always trying to get him to change and never accepting his own interests and needs.

Jason was full of bitter rage with his parents for their failure to take his needs into account, for their autocratic and insensitive discipline, and for the charade of a "happy family" that they tried to perpetuate. He longed to have a family like his friends had, where he saw real sharing, caring, and communication. He agreed with me when I commented about how alienated he felt from his peers, from his own masculinity, or from any sense of being a 17-year-old.

### Looking for normality

After Jason had agreed to start analysis, I learned that he was only applying to universities outside London for the following year. I took up with him the way in which he had already set a termination date on his analysis. Jason said that he could see what I meant by that, but he felt that he also had to get away from his family. There emerged a fantasy that he could achieve a separation from his family by going to a university outside London. Jason's dependency on the achievement of a developmental milestone (e.g. getting into university) as a solution to his feelings of failure to develop towards adulthood was a recurrent theme in the early days of his therapy.

Another theme was Jason's desperate search for "normality" in peers and parents, and his attempts to identify with what he finds, only to feel that he loses contact with any genuine or authentic part of himself in the process. He feels safe when he is conforming. As he said: "I can't remember when I ever lived my own life. It's so far back, I have forgotten. Now, when I like something, I don't even know if it's me, or just what my friends like. I do this so I'll feel okay, feel normal."

One area of his life that he felt enormous shame about was his feeling that he was gay. Eventually, he told me, very painfully, that he never thought about himself as a sexual person—that just never entered his head. He did not mind having girls as friends, but he never thought about being intimate with them sexually. Although I did not say, I had the impression that he was quite anxious about touching his penis, and that he may not have masturbated yet. He appeared to be living, psychically speaking, in a non-sexual body.

During a session, Jason told me: "I don't feel seventeen. I have an image of a seventeen-year-old, and I see my friends that way; but I don't think of myself that way. Like I don't think of my body. I'll go to any extent not to be active." After a thoughtful pause, he continued: "I think of myself more as a child. At home, with grandmother and uncles, I don't feel seventeen. I haven't a clue how to be seventeen. But I think ahead to university, joining clubs and societies, getting a job, and having a family."

I called Jason's attention to his shift to future milestones and fantasies of being normal, and I suggested that his anxiety was aroused by my remark about changes in his body, after he told me that he didn't want to think about his body. Thinking about the future allowed him to get away in fantasy to normal images of himself that did not include his body. Jason now went on at some length about how he has tried to behave with his friends, secretly observing them, picking up clues about how to act, and learning what is acceptable and what is not acceptable.

### A paedophiliac solution

About three weeks later, Jason mentioned to me that he deals with anxieties about his body by never thinking about it.

*Jason*: "But I do get anxious whenever I do sports. Then I choose beginners, like when I go skiing, or I make sure that I'll win, so I won't be embarrassed."

*Analyst*: "Choosing beginners, like choosing to compete with younger children—it sounds like it's difficult for you to think of your own body and your own age."

*Jason*: "Yes, it's younger. My body's younger. I stopped thinking about it at six. But I imagine boys with perfect bodies, thin. But especially their prowess at sports or running." *Then, looking embarrassed, he said quietly*: "When it's possible something might happen, I'm disappointed, and switch off." [*A long silence followed*.] "I imagine someone says, 'You can do that.' I say, 'Show me'."

Jason has now become flushed, and this observation led me to make the following remark:

*Analyst*: "You turn ridicule into sexual excitement."

*Jason*: "No, never sexual excitement." [*He has become very red now*.] "I never ever think of sex. It's only physical prowess. I think of a kiss, but never think of doing it. But it would involve someone. It means getting . . . no, my body is never part of the equation."

At this point, I had the impression that I had enacted something of the homosexual transference with Jason. I felt that I had become intrusive and a part of his sexual excitement. I wondered how he had succeeded in getting me to put his sexual excitement into words. I said: "It sounds like sex or getting involved with someone is dangerous. And you back away." Here I was thinking about his mother's death, and perhaps the feelings and fantasies around her developing cancer after the birth of his younger sibling, but I did not formulate this for Jason at this point.

*Jason*: "I don't even think about it. It's not an issue. I think of being in a family, but never how I'll get there. Like I think of being thin, but not dieting. I think of being thin because that's what would make mother and grandmother happy. So, it would make me happy. I look at what would make them happy, and that's what makes me happy."

*Analyst*: "You mean you don't enjoy your body as it is now."

*Jason*: "In fact, I think of a younger body."

*Analyst*: "That would make them happy, not a seventeen-year-old's body."

*Jason*: "I never think of that."

*Analyst*: "I wonder if there is ridicule in a voice in you that says you can't do it, that you can't have a seventeen-year-old body."

Jason became very still and then sad. I thought he might cry, but he pulled himself together, and he remained silent for the last five minutes of the sessions. After he left, I thought that Jason had somehow abandoned his sexually mature body and had given it over to his mother or father as a passive, inert body, not as a phallic, potent one. My association to the birth of his sibling may be a link to his anxieties about intercourse resulting in not only a new baby, but in the cancer that destroyed his mother. I wondered if this may have contributed to his sense of danger in being heterosexually potent, which then led him to abandon his body at the age of 6. At a more infantile level, Jason's anxieties about development may grow out of his guilt about damage to his mother from his envious attack on her breast after his baby sister was born. This may have contributed to Jason's search for something that would generate sexual feelings in him and would enable him to feel normal without the danger of heterosexual intercourse. Jason's solution was to derive sexual pleasure from another boy's body and from his active use of it.

I was curious about my earlier intervention regarding Jason's turning of ridicule into sexual excitement. It seemed insufficient to explain my reaction entirely in terms of a homosexual scenario—that is, that Jason had seduced me into being phallic and penetrative. It also does not make sense of the clinical material to explain it entirely in terms of Jason's attempt to achieve vicarious gratification and control of dangerous sexual thoughts and feelings by projecting them onto the analyst and thereby experiencing them as located in the analyst.

There is another component that to my mind more fully explains the interaction between patient and analyst—namely, Jason's capacity to keep alive in me and to elicit an image of him as capable of experiencing sexual excitement. Bearing in mind the child's capacity to cue the mother or father in an attempt to "actualize" the "virtual other", this material suggests that Jason, who had been looking for a sense of the norm in his peers, evoked in the transference a parent who thought of him as having a sexual body that was capable of sexual excitement. This provided an opportunity for Jason to think about sexual excitement, something that was previously unshareable. In the intersubjective space between Jason and myself, the potential for a new norm was created.

This experience created a conflict between the family norm of turning a blind eye on sexuality, and a new norm of talking about sexual feelings. Jason resisted change. As long as he remained mentally and physically within his family, he felt normal. However, as his analysis progressed, Jason could acknowledge more readily the disparity between himself and his mates.

*The cost of appearing normal*

Upon his return from a two-week holiday with three male friends, Jason reported that he was very anxious because all they talked about was sex. He had no feelings inside to relate to, and he felt strange and different. He didn't want them to see this. He desperately tried to find excuses and to invent ways to appear normal. Although Jason's shame about being different was evident, he continued to deny any anxiety about sex with girls, or that he ever had any sexual thoughts about his own body. Jason said: "I never thought about any of it, that's why I don't feel anxious."

When Jason left his family and the family norms that he had internalized, he felt strange and different as well as more exposed by a new set of norms, represented by his peers, which allowed expression of sexual fantasies about women and therefore did not protect him from the imagined dangers of intercourse and pregnancy posed by the death of his mother. The absence of a sexual orientation to himself and women felt safer and was, in his family, the norm.

Jason is one of those patients to whom Joyce McDougall was referring in her book *Plea for a Measure of Abnormality* (1980) when she wrote: "Our only hope (and however could we justify it?) would be that this normal person should *come to suffer from his normality*" (p. 472).

# CHAPTER SEVEN

# Vomit as a transitional object

*Em Farrell*

I n this chapter I want to look at one particular aspect of the bulimic ritual—vomit—and its meaning for normal-weight bulimics in relation to the bulimic ritual, as well as its link to early mother–baby experiences and its relevance in the dynamics of the transference and countertransference. The baby, its vomit, the clearing and cleaning-up after vomiting, the baby's faeces— and also material in sessions—may all be seen as attempts to create transitional objects and so construct a bridge towards whole-object relationships and reality.

In the United Kingdom, eating disorders have been understood as being primarily narcissistic in nature, the central problems being the differentiation of self from other, the use of introjective and projective mechanisms, and the move to symbolization. Reiser (1990) describes it thus: "The ultimate roots of bulimic behaviour reach into the earliest stages of life when the mental and the physiological aspects of experience are virtually inseparable" (p. 246).

Winnicott's conceptualization of the area of transitional phenomena and transitional objects creates that much-needed concept, one that can link and be a bridge between the inner and outer worlds, a place where the two interact uninterrupted with the help of the first "not-me" possession, as perceived by the infant, the third area of experience. He says: "The transitional object may therefore stand for the 'external' breast, but *indirectly*, through standing for an 'internal' breast" (Winnicott, 1953a, p. 94). I understand this to mean that an internalized good object has to be present before transitional objects can be found and used, as does a good-enough environment. I think that he is saying that transitional objects can only be used effectively as tools towards whole object relationships if there is a good internalized mother to begin with; for the bulimics, what creates a space for the attempted use of transitional objects is the momentary contact with an internal good and feeding object which occurs during and feelingly after a binge.

An adult with bulimic symptoms can be thought to be re-enacting her earliest and repeated experiences with mother during a binge. From the time of Gull (1874) onwards, the problem of the eating-disordered individual has been seen, in part, as a problem of separation from mother. Otto Sperling (1944) suggested that a mother perceived her psychosomatic child as an extension of her own ego, and Melitta Sperling (1949) suggested that a baby could unconsciously be viewed as representing a hated sibling or parent, or even a hated or wished-for part of the self, particularly a phantasized penis.

Cross (1993) wrote that "Food, feces, menstrual blood, the penis, and finally the fetus can all be experienced as the 'other' within" (p. 59). I want to explore the idea of the mother attempting to use her child's body improperly, as a transitional object for herself, not as a transitional object proper, but as an intermediate object as defined by Kestenberg (1970) and Kestenberg and Weinstein (1988). Their introduction of the term is a modification and expansion of Winnicott's original concept and provides an opportunity to look more closely at precursors to transitional objects.

These authors describe body products and food as being intermediate objects. Such objects are three-dimensional, able to change shape and fuse with the individual's body, and separate from it. They are attached and linked to the baby's body in a way that transitional objects are not. From an observer's point of view, intermediate objects are not given by others to the child, but rather, originate within the body itself. They are linked to particular organs, as vomit is linked to the mouth and faeces is linked to the anus, and these are essential bridges in the development of a secure body image. They are objects that are in themselves transitional to transitional objects. They are not fully transitional because of both their source and their function. They are usually a bridge to mother herself. Unlike true transitional objects, they change and decay quickly. Intermediate objects add an extra stage in the move from the body itself to the use of a piece of blanket or a teddy bear, a stage where, as yet, there is neither a secure internal mother nor a secure body-image.

McDougall (1989) has suggested that if a baby is a mother's sole source of libidinal and narcissistic satisfaction, it will "predispose the adult-to-be to the creation of what I have termed pathological transitional objects of 'transitory objects'" (p. 82). It is feasible that the baby might be seen as a fetish object; indeed, Kestenberg and Weinstein (1988) say of intermediate objects that "They are frequent forerunners of fetishes, whereby the object that stands for the maternal phallus has developed in analogy to the shape of the fecal column" (p. 91). A baby cannot be thought to be an intermediate or transitional object in that it has its own life and does not change in the way either intermediate or transitional objects do. Some mothers—those whose own internal body image is insecure—use their baby as though it were both an intermediate and a transitional object. They do not know the difference.

The bulimic ritual is usually described as bingeing on food, followed by self-induced vomiting. Sometimes laxatives are taken. However, the ritualistic element of the bulimic act does not usually end here. It goes on. It goes on during the time of clearing up, and cleaning up. I wish to look at the role that vomit plays during this time, using Winnicott's ideas of transitional objects to understand this neglected and rarely talked-about part of the ritual.

In the clinical extract that follows, I want to underline the vomit, the environment, and the cleaning-up process in particular. It was written in the third person by a normal-weight bulimic:

"The substance in her mouth had long since stopped tasting of the biscuit it had once been. The first dozen or so after the bread had been good, but now the taste had changed into a bland nothingness. She saw herself reaching for the packet again, but she was unable to stop, although she knew that food was not the answer. She chewed hard, sucked at the paste, forced herself to swallow and by then another biscuit had found its way into her mouth. She had no choice but to go on until the packet was empty. She felt grounded, as if her stomach had taken her over. Limbs felt as insubstantial as spiders' legs, her stomach enveloped her. It spread from her knees, and up to her heart, which was pumping hard, struggling with the burden imposed on it, and her lungs were screaming for air, but food seemed to fill up all the spaces. She needed to breathe normally, and didn't want to risk blocking the plumbing again. She found herself outside. No one was about. She thrust her fingers violently to the back of her throat. Her whole body shook as the food, like a stammering eruption, came out of her. She had not bothered to take her shoes off and they were now splattered with vomit along with her clothes. She noticed, and thought as she had before how strange it was that what you ate last did not necessarily come up first. The bile in her mouth was unpleasant, but she could breathe again. She was lighter and somehow affirmed, and could now get back to her normality. She saw with a mixture of pride and disgust the evidence on the ground before her, the piles of vomit from different occasions in various states of decay—biodegradable at least, she thought, and part of herself. She returned to the house in a dream state, to clean herself up, and left the garden behind."

This account illustrates some elements of what has not been explored—namely, the period that occurs after the vomiting, as well as the vomit itself, and how the transition is made from bingeing and vomiting back to normal life. The vomit almost seems to have a life of its own.

I offer four clinical vignettes to elucidate some of the possible meanings of vomit. David Krueger (1988) has written:

> These individuals, because of their concrete, non-symbolic mode of operation, are not able to move to an external non-bodily transitional object. They seem instead to struggle to *create* a transitional object which *is* external, concrete, and spe-

cific. The effectiveness of the object is fleeting, however, and can remain no more fixed in emotional consciousness than the defective internal images of body, self or other. [pp. 61–62]

David Krueger is using the term "transitional" where I would use the word "intermediate" due to its transitory nature, its creation within the body, and its role in helping to define and restore a more complete internal body-image. This is a very particular and rare use of vomit. Normal-weight and anorexic bulimics may have many different phantasies about their vomit, at different stages in their illness and on different days. Vomit can be thought about more generally as being an intermediate object, as with Patient F described below. It is disposed of and is one of the many stages of their bulimic ritual. These patients use the ritual in an attempt to integrate and validate their body image, but what is rare is the attempt to use vomit as a transitional object—for these patients have failed, as have their mothers before them, to differentiate between intermediate and transitional objects. They turn to their body products, their intermediate objects, and try to turn them into transitional objects proper, which they can keep and use and play with for as long as they need. For Winnicott (1967), one of the crucial features of transitional objects and transitional phenomena is a certain quality that we possess in ourselves when we observe these objects and phenomena. Bear this in mind when reading about the four patients described below.

> Patient E worked in an office and she did not enjoy her job or her surroundings. She was extremely creative and used her skills to earn extra pocket money away from the office. Whilst at work, she would sit at her desk and, whenever she could, would eat—biscuits, sandwiches, chocolate bars. She made them last all day long. She would eat something, and then for an hour or two hours afterwards she would ruminate, bringing the food back up into her mouth where it would be chewed and swallowed again. This happened without her conscious awareness, although she could prevent it happening when she wanted or needed to.

\* \* \*

Patient C was a very fit, normal-weight bulimic. She lived at home with her mother and sisters. Her mother locked up the food at certain times during the day to try to stop her from bingeing. This failed, and C would binge secretly in her room. She kept the packaging and wrappers of the food she ate. When she had finished bingeing, she would not go to the bathroom to be sick, as she was too frightened of being caught. She would vomit into plastic bags in her bedroom, which she then placed either in her wardrobe, in her chest of drawers, or under her bed. She did dispose of the vomit-filled bags, but not at the first opportunity, which meant there was always more than one bag of vomit in her room.

* * *

Patient F was a normal-weight bulimic who binged and vomited many times a day. She did not feel able to work. After bingeing, she would make herself sick. Sometimes the action would be very violent and the vomit would splatter back into her face, around the lavatory, and onto her clothes and shoes. She would then spend time carefully cleaning up herself and the bathroom. She took numerous laxatives on a daily basis, and after a bowel movement or movements she would change her clothes if necessary and wash her body with care.

* * *

Patient M was a normal-weight bulimic who ate compulsively on a fairly regular basis. She worked in a hotel and did shift work. Sometimes she would binge and vomit, normally in the evening before going to bed. After bingeing and vomiting, she would then eat again, until she felt full, at which point she would lie down and go to sleep. She would be aware of the food inside her, and she would also be aware of her body shape on the bed as she was going to sleep. She would often report dream-like images before slipping into sleep.

For Patient E, the experience of partially digested food, which was chewed and swallowed, and chewed and swallowed again, helped to assuage her anxiety. The vomit was available, and she played with it in her mouth, and this provided a third area of experiencing which removed her from an awareness of the barrenness of her inner and outer worlds. She could stay at work as a result. It proved itself to be enabling and was for her a transitional object.

For Patient C, both her vomit and the remnants of food in the form of its wrappings and packaging were there for her to use as transitional objects, but for a limited time only. They were moved around the room, felt, played with, thrown away. In a bag, vomit has all the sensory requirements of a transitional object, a smell, a texture, a mobility, and a life of its own. However, it is not a transitional object, because it came from within her body, and decayed. It had to be thrown away after a certain time, as it began to grow mould.

Going to sleep with a blanket in one hand is not unusual for a baby. So, too for Patient M, who could sleep once her transitional object of food was inside her. This is different from the sleepiness of the compulsive eater, for it was related to the vomit that had already been expelled and in fantasy, hunger, and destruction had been dealt with. The good mother had been experienced and the bad mother had gone. Then came the time for something to play with, to feel in a safe place with, which enabled her to sleep.

For Patient F, the clearing-up process itself was soothing and provided an important in-between stage that enabled her to return to reality. This use of the post-vomit time as a transitional arena is a common, though rarely talked about, part of the bulimic ritual, for many normal weight and anorexic bulimics.

Vomit is used in all these examples, apart from that of Patient M, as though it were a transitional object, rather than an intermediate object. More commonly, vomit is used as an intermediate object to clarify body boundaries, and the cleaning-up ritual is used as though it were a transitional object. It is used to return to a world of whole-object relating and perhaps provides the one area where a semblance of Winnicott's third area of experiencing is appreciated, however painfully. It becomes a bridge back to reality. For Patient M, bingeing and vomiting, and then eating again, allowed her to go to sleep. For Patient E, ruminating enabled her to stay and to perform at work.

It must not be forgotten that viewing the bulimic ritual as being a way to create and use transitional objects is only one way of understanding it—a way that adds a more benign understanding to a ritual usually thought of as being primarily destructive. The less well the individual, the more likely she is to try using vomit as a transitional object. The same may apply to individuals who abuse laxatives excessively and in phantasy thus speed up and control the production of faeces, with which they become overly preoccupied. In some cases, they become attached to the often painful and time-consuming process of evacuation and clearing-up.

I want to use the idea of baby-vomit or faeces as intermediate objects in a metaphorical way to understand some of the pressures that the psychotherapist will experience in the transference, which include pressures to behave in a neglectful or sadistic fashion. Within the transference, the likelihood is of being expected to be a brutalizing and misunderstanding mother, a mother who is only there to use her child/patient for her own needs and who cannot understand, contain, or process any of the patient's material. It might, as well, be shit or vomit. Often, the unconscious aim of the patient is to be invaded, to feel controlled, so that no separation is known or experienced. There is in effect no space to play or think. This is a point made indirectly by Cross (1993), who has written that "Internal and external sadomasochism are linked through the common element of the body; other people are manipulated as if they were extensions of the body, and functions or parts of the body are tyrannized as if they were unruly persons" (p. 62). Rizzuto (1988) has suggested that "In the countertransference the analyst experiences exhaustion, discouragement, anger, humiliation, and a wish to get rid of the patient" (p. 372). The clinician may wish to throw the patient up and out. This chaos has to be tolerated if progress is to be made (Boris, 1984).

The psychotherapist has to become what the child felt the mother could never be—a container and processor of the patient's feelings, thoughts, and terrifying anxieties. The expectation is to receive them back in an amplified and frightening form, and this is what the psychotherapist has to try to avoid, namely regurgitation. The patient expects to be force-fed or starved, and she tries to do the same to the clinician. The vomit has to be accepted as worthwhile material, however incoherent, disconnected, or fractured it may seem. At some stage, the time comes when it is possible to use countertransference feelings to make sense of the material and to allow an interpretation to be given a hearing, however briefly.

The bulimic ritual *is* a ritual, and the necessity of repetition means that although vomit may be used by some bulimics as a transitional object, the lack of a stabilized good internal object means that the move to the use of a transitional object that is not of the self, and made by the self, remains unachievable. Perhaps the storms in the treatment, the attacks made by bulimics on the psychotherapist, can be understood as an attempt to revive a link; once this has been survived, work can take place in the transitional space. This occurs in the aftermath of the bingeing through the acceptance of the vomit, sometimes projectile, which occurs within the psychotherapeutic relationship. The vomit has to be accepted as a gift, and like a transitional object, it must not be questioned or taken away until its use has faded into insignificance. Metaphorical vomiting is being used in the psychotherapeutic relationship as a way of creating a space, and this space must be understood and protected if these patients are to move towards whole-object relationships. This move, in turn, facilitates the existence of an effective digestive tract in their internal world.

# CHAPTER EIGHT

# Transitional objects in the treatment of primitive mental states

*Peter Giovacchini*

The field of mental health is in a state of transition, a fact that makes Winnicott's works even more relevant. Winnicott (1953a) was the first to introduce the concepts of the transitional object and transitional space, which helped pave the pathway from the world of the intrapsychic to that of object relationships.

Freud acknowledged but did not particularly emphasize the role of the external milieu in the production of psychopathology. Discussing severe psychopathology, he did not rely exclusively on an intrapsychic focus but stressed conflicts between the ego and the outer world (Freud, 1924b [1923], 1924e). Previously, he had formulated childhood seductions as aetiologic traumas in the causation of obsessive compulsive and hysterical neuroses (Freud, 1894a, 1896b), but later he returned to the intrapsychic perspective in that he believed most of these alleged seductions were, in fact, fantasies (Freud, 1906c).

Melanie Klein purported to be more Freudian than Freud. Though she recognized that there was an external world and caregivers, most of her explorations and formulations concerned the internal world and internal objects as they are subjected to introjective and projective mechanisms. The most attention given to an interaction that is not exclusively confined to the boundaries of the mind was based on projective identification (Klein, 1946), which referred to the temporary relinquishment of an impulse or part of the mind as it is projected into the analyst. This can be, among other things, a developmental experience, in which case it would highlight the participation of the external world in intrapsychic integration and maturation. This was about the only attention she gave to interpersonal experiences.

Almost everything about the psyche could be explained by the death instinct, according to Klein. An inherent destructive force drives the psyche to feeling greed, envy, and guilt and finally to the paranoid–schizoid and depressive positions.

Winnicott was known as representing a third orientation, between Melanie Klein and Anna Freud, who shared her father's viewpoint. Actually, I do not believe he belonged to a continuum between the Klein–Freud polarity. Rather, I conjecture that Winnicott modified and moved away from Klein in order to maintain both an intrapsychic and object-relationship focus. Though he straddled between transactions with the external world and those occurring exclusively within the psyche, he introduced novel ideas in his construction of the concepts of transitional objects and transitional space. Regarding the paranoid–schizoid and depressive positions, he altered Klein's language to make them more palatable, but his formulations regarding transitional phenomena are unique and, in my opinion, pivotal to our understanding of psychic development, and they have important implications regarding psychopathology and the therapeutic process.

The classical analyst has fought valiantly for the preservation of instinct theory. Anna Freud (1965) criticized Richard Sterba (1934) when he introduced the concept of the self-observing ego because it was diverting attention away from the id. I was somewhat surprised when Winnicott told me that he did not place much importance on his construction of the transitional object, and he could not understand why Anna Freud was so taken by it. Evidently, she believed that it was an extremely important contribution, especially to a psychoanalytically derived theory of infant development, whereas Winnicott, at least initially, was inclined to underplay it.

### Developmental vicissitudes, symbiosis, and transitional phenomena

Instinct theory has receded into the background, decathected so to speak, as clinicians encounter an increasing number of patients who are suffering from defects in character structure rather than intrapsychic conflict. These patients tend to have extremely traumatic backgrounds that have made the course of emotional development difficult and painful. The antecedents of their psychopathology are found in developmental defects. The transitional objects and space are also involved in psychopathological processes and are defectively constructed.

Klein wrote about emotional development as if it occurred *sui generis*—that is, without interactions with the external world. I doubt that she would have denied the significance of the nurturing interaction, but she certainly did not stress it. Winnicott's formulations about the transitional space give us important insights as to the sequence of psychic maturation and as to how the child enters the outer world. Again, I doubt that he would have accepted the extent of his contribution, but I believe it is quite extensive.

Within the last several decades, there has been considerable emphasis on fusion and merging. Mahler and Furer (1968) have stressed that separation–individuation occurs when the infant "hatches" from a symbiotic fusion state with the mother. This is theoretically unfeasible because the construction of a state of symbiotic fusion requires at least some minimal recognition of an external object in order to be able to effect a merger. Clearly, this is inconsistent because the ability to recognize the external world as separate from the self, according to Mahler and others, presupposes a state of fusion that, in itself, is the outcome of some minimal separation and individuation.

I believe that the establishment of transitional phenomena helps us resolve this dilemma and leads to insights about developmental processes that are instrumental to the child's construction of and entrance into the external world. Winnicott's ideas about transitional states are also relevant to the understanding of psychopathological processes.

Freud (1915c) wrote about the succession of various stages of psychosexual development, comparing them to waves of lava overlapping as they flow downhill. He was describing that early developmental phases are carried forward, to some extent, into later psychic states. The smoother the continuity of developmental progression, the greater the cohesion of the self representation and its movement into and adaptations to the external world.

For clinicians, it is especially important to explore the transition from early states of emotional organization to later reality-adapted, secondary-process-organized development levels. The vicissitudes that occur at these junctures would have significant impact on the degree and quality of psychopathology as it affects character structure.

I briefly review below the concepts of transitional objects and phenomena because, although much has been written about them, they are still difficult to understand. After thoroughly reading Winnicott, I was still somewhat confused and did not feel that I had an adequate overview of his compelling and intriguing but to some extent puzzling ideas. I wanted to understand Winnicott's poetry better, and although I had exchanged letters with him, I felt a personal visit was necessary for my full comprehension.

To recapitulate, Winnicott (1953a) believed that the infant initially believes that he is the source of his own nurture, a mental organization that is characterized by what he calls primary psychic creativity. The mother, because of her total psychological and even biological involvement with her child, a state that Winnicott (1956a) called primary maternal preoccupation, supports the child's illusion of self-sufficiency. The child is involved primarily with the regulation and gratification of needs without any particular awareness of the caregiver's contribution, according to Winnicott. Winnicott added that later the child enjoys the illusion of being the source of its own nurture and can play with it, indicating that the child has recognized it as an illusion.

I believe that the recognition of an illusion and its playful manipulation indicates a beginning recognition of the external world, an early separation–individuation that does not involve being merged and evolving from such a fusion.

The adult's and child's viewpoints during these early phases are asymmetrical. Although the mother and the infant need each other, their relationship is not symbiotic except on the surface. The mother needs the child for her psychological survival, and the child needs the mother for its total—that is, emotional and physical—existence but is not aware of it before separation–individuation. Thus, there is an asymmetry regarding psychological awareness.

Correspondingly, the mother's and child's views of the surrounding space are different. The mother, at some level, knows where her boundaries end and where those of the infant begin; but the child, according to Winnicott, does not as yet accept any limitations to the boundaries of the self. Where the mother's boundaries intrude into the child's space defines the transitional space. Any objects—that is, objects from the adult's perceptions—represent parts of the self to the child.

Winnicott views the infant as omnipotent in this early preobject phase, having an illusion of controlling the universe. This, in my mind, is part of Winnicott's poetry, which attributes qualities to the infant that are clearly beyond the level of development. These are adultomorphic descriptions of early attempts at self-regulation and the maintenance of homeostatic equilibrium.

I asked Winnicott if we could assume that the infant had been successful in establishing a nurturing matrix—that is, an endopsychic representation of a gratifying nursing experience. This would lead to a state of inner calm that is later reflected in enhanced self-esteem and confidence. The actual objects in the transitional space become endowed with this nurturing matrix and become transitional objects, but they are still parts of the self.

As the child plays with the transitional object in a space that initially is considered as being part of the psychic domain, it begins to understand the nature of illusion, which means that it is becoming able to distinguish the inner from the outer world. The well-equilibrated child deals with the external world in an illusory fashion—that is, everything is made into an enjoyable game. The transitional space may recede as reality demands become greater, but it correspondingly expands with a sense of well-being and creative, adventurous excursions into unknown areas of the external world. This becomes a learning and growth experience.

There is a back-and-forth movement between increasingly differentiated perceptions of the surrounding milieu and external objects, and the child incorporates them in the psyche as parts of the self. The latter represent fusion or merger, but it is the outcome of separation–individuation rather than its precursor.

As the psyche continues differentiating, interpersonal relationships become less and less asymmetrical. The self representation achieves synthesis and cohesion, transactions with external objects tend towards symmetry, and the capacity for intimacy develops. The ultimate expression of intimacy is a fusion with a loving and beloved person, which among adults is expressed sexually. This is a situation of mutual dependency (Giovacchini, 1958), a true state of symbiosis in which similar needs and gratifications are expressed by both partners. Though they can submerge and lose themselves in a state of fusion, they emerge with a heightened sense of autonomy. There is both mutual dependency and mutual gratification within the context of progressive emotional maturation and the achievement of states of higher psychic synthesis.

Viewing the construction of the transitional space as an essential aspect of the developmental process maintains an intrapsychic focus without excluding the role of external objects in promoting emotional maturation. It also stresses their role, when advanced developmental levels have been achieved, in maintaining autonomy, self-esteem, and intimacy.

A middle-aged woman entered therapy without any sense of an individual identity. She viewed herself as an "as-if" character (Deutsch, 1942) and felt that, emotionally speaking, she had been submerged by her mother and brother. She also considered herself as an appendage to her therapist, and in her marriage her husband constantly berated her for being a non-entity and otherwise verbally abused her.

Her mother had been able to provide gratification, and, to the degree that she did, as a child the patient was able to function quite adequately and developed some sense of identity, but she let herself be submerged (Giovacchini, 1964, 1972). As her second analyst, I believed that she was a "pseudo-as-if", rather than an "as-if" character. The gratification she received, however, occurred in an ambivalent setting. The lullabies her mother sang to soothe her referred to babies dying or being abandoned. She was pushed into the background in favour of a younger brother.

She vividly recalled an episode during childhood when a family photograph was being taken, but she was not included in it. To add insult to injury, her mother took her doll and gave it temporarily to her brother so that it could be included in the photograph. Later, she was forced to care for her brother, especially when he was expressing his needs for autonomy. For example, she had to pick up his toys when he threw them out of the crib. Her childhood was in no way as traumatic as those that clinicians frequently encounter in the histories of physically and sexually abused children. Still, she felt that there was an arrest in character development, especially in the construction of the self representation.

The doll, a transitional object, represented her budding infantile self. She felt as if she had been robbed of her potential identity. An essential part of herself was given to her brother, but more important was that her developmental mode was taken away from her. Instead of the family being concerned about her growing up, she was relegated to the background and had to be available to others. As a child, she was put in the service of her brother's development; as an adult, she was made responsible for the psychic cohesion of her husband.

Her first analyst ultimately committed suicide, and she felt that she had failed him. She started working for a suicide hotline, making herself available to others at the expense of her needs and individuality. To a large extent, that is how she viewed her analysis—that she did not exist as a separate being. She felt fused with her analyst but subservient to his needs. He was depressed, as was her husband.

Fusion did not represent a progressive, intimate symbiotic attachment. It was a recapitulation of an adaptive modality that was forced upon her during childhood, one that caused her, relatively speaking, to arrest the course of emotional development, but it, nevertheless, permitted her to survive. It was a defence against her mother's unconscious need to abandon or kill her, as depicted in the lullaby she sang while feeding her. I suspect, however, that the persons she fused with—that is, her analyst and her husband—had similar maldevelopments of the self representation. They were perhaps masked by depression. The patient as a child fused with her mother, presumably as a defence against the fear of abandonment and as a protection against her mother's unconscious hostility towards her. Fusion, as an adaptive modality, was characterologically manifested in as-if qualities.

The psyche, after it has reached a certain level of maturation, seeks external objects, as Fairbairn (1941) has stressed. As stated, the self representation is replenished and self-esteem enhanced in states of intimate symbiotic fusion. As fusion can be drawn into the service of psychopathology, the symbiotic nature of the relationship is distorted for defensive purposes. This is most likely to happen when the infantile milieu has been extremely traumatic.

We hear a good deal today about co-dependence, a term that I believe confuses more than it clarifies. It signifies mutual dependence—that is, symbiosis—but it concentrates only on surface interactions, ignoring deeper levels of the personality, transitional phenomena, and the complex reactions between intrapsychic processes and the external world.

The psyche's propensity towards states of symbiotic merger has significant implications for normal development as well as for psychopathology. In order to successfully fuse with an external object, the self representations involved must *de facto* be similar. Otherwise, a smooth, cohesive union could not occur and each partner would experience the other as a foreign body, necessitating defensive distancing manoeuvres.

The similarities of symbiotic partners might not be at the manifest level. One partner in a long-lasting but not necessarily stable relationship may be sadistic, the other masochistic, but basically their character structures are similar, and if there is psychopathology, it is equivalent. As I have indicated (Giovacchini, 1958, 1965, 1967), schizophrenics marry schizophrenics, hysterics marry hysterics—an equivalence that is especially prevalent among alcoholics.

Alcoholics have relationships based on complementarity. One partner drinks, and the other is long-suffering but condescendingly deprecating.

One evening, a husband brought his wife, a patient of mine, to my front door to show me how drunk she was. The patient felt utterly humiliated. It was learned that early in the marriage the husband was constantly drunk, to the extent that he had to be hospitalized because the family was afraid he would accidentally kill himself, as in an automobile accident. At that time, his wife was viciously cruel and deprecating, just as he now was. The similarities of character structure and psychopathology, however, were evident in the role reversals.

Another patient, the wife of a professional man, had many phobias, such as fear of travelling and heights and not being able to be more than twenty feet away from a toilet. Because of these phobias, she was blamed by her husband for their complete lack of social life. The latter was important to him because his upward mobility was dependent upon being able to form good social relationships with his superiors. His wife was able to overcome her symptoms, and the husband then developed exactly the same phobias. His symptoms were apparently covered up by hers. In as much as she inhibited his mobility, he did not have to face potentially frightening, conflictful situations. He could hide behind her psychopathology, but, basically, they had similar problems.

At times, as these patients illustrate, the ego states of symbiotic partners radically and abruptly change; there is a sudden role reversal. The state of fusion is unstable in terms of its polarities and, thereby, differs from the symbiosis characteristic of healthy intimacy. In the latter, there is a blending, a union, a transcendental and creative experience that enhances the totality of the self representation, whereas in these instances of psychopathology there is usually a complementary fusion. Various fragments of each partner's self representation fuse with each other. It is a fragmented fusion, emphasizing character discontinuity and a lack of smooth transitions, rather than being one based on a cohesive, harmonious blending.

Smooth transitions between various ego states, or, during childhood, between different developmental levels, are the outcome of well-constructed transitional spaces and objects. This would appear self-evident, but this correlation has many implications. Severely disturbed patients, including schizophrenics, do not demonstrate an orderly sequence of developmental stages that contribute to the breadth and integrity of the self representation as well as its continuity. These patients are fragmented, and their reactions and orientations may be inconsistent and so contradictory at times that they seem to be different people. They have suffered from the impacts of a traumatic, cruel, and abusive infantile environment.

I am not referring to multiple personalities, a subject that I consider controversial. Rather, I am stressing a group of patients who are unable to deal with transitional experiences and with the discontinuity of character and other character defects that create a bizarre and confusing clinical picture. Some patients cannot tolerate change. They find it difficult to accept the analyst's vacations and find the time between sessions intolerable. They have problems keeping various frames of references separate or moving from one to another.

> I recall a young divorced woman who began treatment by asking me when I would be away on trips. She had to know the exact dates and the details of where I would be. She also had to have telephone numbers so that she could get in touch with me. She had no ability to hold mental representations of persons unless they were in a familiar environment. Placing the external object in a different setting meant losing it because her psyche was unable to switch frames of reference. It could not make transitions.

Winnicott (1949a) believed that some patients evoked uncomfortable and hostile reactions in their therapists. These responses are part of the analytic interaction and can lead to important insights about psychopathology and treatment techniques. The analyst often finds solace knowing that there will be an end to the session and an adequate fee. Relief is obtained when there is a change in frames of reference, a shift from the analytic setting to the analyst's personal world in which the patient does not belong, or perhaps to the different setting of the next patient.

The patient, on the other hand, does not accept or tolerate transitions. Frequently, these patients manifest their intolerance of transitions by refusing to leave at the end of the session, and, understandably, this can cause a serious dilemma for the therapist, one that has no clear-cut solution.

I once told a patient that she would have to leave promptly when her time was up, otherwise I would be thinking throughout her session how I was going to cope with her refusal to leave. This would be unfair to her because I should be giving my full attention to her associations rather than worrying about her behaviour regarding ending the session. In this instance, it worked, but there are situations where nothing the therapist said would have any effect.

The extreme occasion is when security has to be called and the patient physically ejected, an unfortunate and humiliating experience for both patient and therapist. These patients often view their surroundings in a highly concrete fashion. For them, their milieu is unidimensional, a black-and-white world without any grey areas. Their world is bleak and devoid of fantasy and other elements that are the outcome of intrapsychic processes.

As stated, they lack or have a defective transitional space. The capacity for illusion does not develop, and they are stuck, so to speak, in a narrow, constricted, concrete frame of reference. They cling to a mechanistically constructed universe, because they cannot comprehend any other.

## Summary and conclusions

Clearly, the concepts of the transitional space and transitional phenomena are vital for our understanding of patients whose psychopathology is based on structural defects, who are most frequently encountered in clinical practice. Such concepts explain the course of emotional development, especially how the child enters the external world and how the process of separation and individuation occurs. Defects in the path of emotional development lead to specific symptomatic, characterological, and behavioural aberrations that are found in the majority of the concretely orientated patients so commonly seen by clinicians.

These patients' capacity for intimate relationships is limited. Symbiotic fusion is not enhancing. Rather, they form relationships that support their psychopathology. The clinical examples demonstrate in a lasting relationship the persons involved suffer from similar types of psychopathology. These are not comfortable or intimate unions. Rather, through symbiosis, they support a psychopathological equilibrium.

The lack of a transitional space, or the presence of a defective transitional space, can lead to an inability to endure transitional experiences. These patients demand constancy in their environment, and they need to know where and when they can find their caregivers and other supportive persons, because they cannot hold mental representations without the presence of the external object—a lack of the evocative (Fraiberg, 1969).

This intolerance to transition can lead to technical problems, a particularly vexing example being when the patient refuses to leave at the end of the hour. Another special treatment difficulty often is the patient's degree of concreteness, a lack of psychological-mindedness, a quality that has been considered to be essential for psychoanalytic treatment. This again points to the importance of transitional phenomena. Winnicott stressed that the capacity for illusion develops in the transitional space. This is the site of creative accomplishments and the construction of fantasy and self-contemplation, qualities that are the essence of psychological-mindedness and the psychoanalytic interaction.

Nevertheless, many concretely orientated patients can be treated in a psychoanalytic context. By establishing a holding environment (Giovacchini, 1993) and the internalization of the analyst's mode of perceiving, the patient gradually begins to develop a transitional state. This is a topic that needs to be developed further as psychoanalysis continues to expand its horizons.

# CHAPTER NINE

# D. W. Winnicott and the understanding of sexual perversions

*Charles Socarides*

Winnicott's clinical work with infants and children in the pre-oedipal phase of development, and his observations on the dynamic relationship between mother and child have proven to be an important source of information for the elucidation of the origins of those ineluctable conditions, the sexual perversions. His concepts of good-enough mothering and of the true self and false self, his idea that there is no such thing as a baby, only a nursing couple, as well as his important discovery of the concept of the transitional object, all shed much light on the development of the perversions.

While I have utilized primarily the theoretical framework suggested by Margaret Mahler and her associates (cf. Mahler, 1966, 1974; Mahler & Furer, 1968; Mahler, Pine, & Bergman, 1975) on the theory of separation–individuation, as well as the work of René Spitz (1959) and the writings of object relations theorists, notably Otto Kernberg (1975), in support of my clinical findings, my writings over four decades on sexual perversions have been greatly enriched by Winnicott's theories, observations, and conclusions.

In this chapter, I describe several areas in which I have applied some of Winnicott's concepts to material derived from the analysis and reconstruction of the early life of perverse patients, namely (1) the false-self integration found in the perverse patient, (2) the non-facilitating environment in which the patient was raised, and (3) the infantile genetic matrix of the patient's depressive affect and its importance in perverse development. My findings on these several issues derive from the psychoanalytic study of obligatory perverse patients (Pre-oedipal Type I and Pre-oedipal Type II homosexual patients) and other individuals (Socarides, 1978, 1988). The individual psychopathology, the symptom picture, and the ego deficits that one finds in perverse patients have their roots in these early disturbances and derailments.

## False-self integration in perverse individuals

My theoretical approach to perverse patients is a combination of the Mahlerian theory of separation–individuation (cf. Mahler et al., 1975), the "maturational compliance" theory of Spitz (1959), and the concepts of true self and false self, as espoused by Winnicott (1960c). In perverse individuals, the facilitating process that Winnicott described is derailed as the mother does not respond appropriately to her male child's developmental need for intrapsychic separation during the separation–individuation phases of development. The result is a failure of individuation, separation, and autonomy and a later disturbance in the promotion of object constancy. As a consequence, I wish to suggest that a false-self organization emerges that consists largely of an introjection of the mother.

It is beyond the scope of his paper to describe the true-self and false-self organizations so carefully delineated by Winnicott. Although my use of these terms is not identical to that of Winnicott, I believe my description falls within the basic definitions supplied by Moore and Fine (1990):

> The true self evolves its idiom through a maternal care that supports the child's continuity of being, enabling the child to generate an expressive life from a core of self authorized by his or her sense of personal reality. . . . The false self, like the ego,

is a stable and recurring, continuously operated structure. . . . True and false self thus refer not to a moral order, but to qualities in self–other experiences that support spontaneous expression (true self), or reactive living (false self). [p. 209]

The male child who has introjected the mother responds with excessive clinging to the mother in infancy and early childhood, and he experiences severe anxiety of both fragmentation and separation which may continue throughout life. There are merging and fusion phenomena, fears of the engulfing mother, faulty body-ego images, disturbances in self-concept, and an inability to modulate aggression because of the difficulty in adequately separating from her. There may be a consequent inability to appreciate body-space relationships, a finding frequently seen in perverse individuals.

As early as 1960, in his essay "Ego Distortion in Terms of True and False Self", Winnicott (1960c) described the defensive nature of the false self, whose function is to "hide and protect the true self" (p. 146), and he classified several false-self organizations. At one extreme, the false self "sets up as real and it is this that observers tend to think is the real person" (p. 142). I contend that what is lacking in all those with obligatory sexual perversions is an appropriate gender-defined self-identity in accordance with anatomy. This is the core problem in all perverse patients. In line with Winnicott's suggestion, this is a false-self organization as it has as its positive aim the preservation of the individual in spite of the abnormal environmental conditions that it had met previously, but had failed to overcome. The achievement of a true-self organization, which includes a gender-defined self-organization appropriate to the anatomy, becomes the aim of all psychoanalytic treatment of sexual perversions.

To recapitulate, the perverse false-self organization is one in which a false personality exists in the form of a continuation of the *primary feminine identification with the mother* (Jacobson, 1946; Kestenberg, 1956; Lampl-de Groot, 1946; Socarides, 1960, 1974; van der Leeuw, 1958), overlaying and obscuring the original core gender identity of the child. This is a continuation of the original passive relationship with the mother—that is, an *active feminine pre-oedipal identification*. Such a primitive identification expresses itself in very primitive perverse fantasies: the feeling that one is part female, the wish for female genitalia, the wish for a child, and so forth. In such children, for example, the wish to bear a child (frequently found in the analysis of fetishists: Kestenberg, 1956; Socarides, 1960; van der Leeuw, 1958) is experienced as an act of achievement bringing deep satisfaction and demonstrating that one is "like mother" and as powerful as she is. As adults in analysis, such patients display pre-oedipal material in which they behave in a childish fashion, and remembering is often replaced by acting out. Such an identification does not consist of passive feminine wishes for the father in order to take the mother's place secondary to the oedipal conflict (an example of secondary identification arising from oedipal rivalry) or the pressure of castration fear, but represents the creation of a false self, imitative of and identified with the maternal figure.

The persistence of this identification is a monument to the failure of disidentification with the mother, and an inability to form a counter-identification with the paternal figure (Greenson, 1968; Socarides, 1988). This false self is present in the conscious and/or unconscious of all sexual perverts, and it is especially obvious in overt obligatory homosexuals and transvestites and in transsexual individuals. The retention of the primary feminine identification with the mother, and the fixation that results, may occur at various levels of separation–individuation, whether during the rapprochement, differentiation, or practising sub-phases. The earlier the fixation (e.g. in the differentiating and practising sub-phases), the more severe is the inability to separate the "I" from the "Thou", and the greater the anxiety and the guilt will be upon attempting a separation. All in all, however, the false gender-defined self-identity that has ensued protects the individual from severe regression and from engulfment by the maternal figure, and the perverse acts are a means of salvation from further engulfment.

Under these conditions, the mother does not allow appropriate cathexis of external objects, and, in Winnicott's (1960c) words, "the infant lives, but lives falsely" (p. 146). The false self of the pervert reacts to the environmental demands "and the infant seems to accept them" (p. 146) through his primary identification with the mother. As Winnicott noted: "Through this False Self the infant builds up a false set of relationships, and by means of introjection even attains a show of being real, so that the child may grow to be just like mother, nurse, aunt, brother, or whoever at the same time dominates the scene" (p. 146). In these individuals, Winnicott wrote that "Compliance is the main feature, with imitation as a speciality" (p. 147).

All in all, in patients with obligatory perversions, a psychological development has taken place which is not age-adequate for a given critical period of separation–individuation, and there is a distortion in the development of a true self. It is therefore difficult, if not impossible, for an individual to acquire a true self at a later stage. This is because, as Spitz (1959) noted, "at the appropriate critical period, a given item of psychological development will find all the maturational conditions [un]favourable for its establishment" (p. 101). Spitz referred to the positive aspects of this situation as "maturational compliance", similar to Winnicott's "maturational process". The counterpart to maturational compliance is "developmental (psychological) compliance". There must be "a synchronicity of maturation and development . . . [as] an essential feature of normal development" (Spitz, 1959, p. 84).

Spitz (1959) observed that

> If, during the critical period, the appropriate (psychological) development is not forthcoming, then the maturation factors will seize on other (psychological) developmental items available. These developmental items will be modified and distorted until they comply with maturation needs, and integration will be established which deviates from the norm. . . . As a result, when the bypassed (psychological) developmental item finally does become available at a later stage, he will find the maturational positions occupied by compensating, though deviant, structures and unavailable for normal integration. [p. 76]

I conclude that such deviant structures, in my opinion, may also be considered false-self structures. The observations of Margaret Mahler, René Spitz, and Donald Winnicott as regards maturation, synchronicity, and integration have much in common, as noted above, and all can well be applied to many of the problems of the early development of perverse individuals. For example, the homosexual has failed to make the intrapsychic separation from the mother at the proper stage of development. As a result, there remains a chronic intrapsychic fixation point to which he remains fixed, despite having passed through other developmental maturational phases with some success. In these maturational positions, there have been compensating and deviant structures formed to compensate for the infantile deficiency. These structures are intimately concerned with problems of identity (gender-defined self-identity), faulty ego boundaries, introjective and projective anxieties, fears of invasion and engulfment, separation and fragmentation anxieties, disturbances in the capacity to form object relations, as well as the creation of a false-self integration.

## Failures of the maturational processes in deviant patients

In his essay "Psychiatric Disorder in Terms of Infantile Maturational Processes", Winnicott (1963d) stated his major theoretical concept succinctly:

> In infancy the growth-process belongs to the infant, and is the sum of inherited tendencies, and this includes the *maturational process*. The maturational process only takes effect in an individual infant in so far as there is a *facilitating environment*. The study of the facilitating environment is almost as important at the beginning as the study of the individual maturational process. The characteristic of the maturational process is the drive towards *integration*, which comes to mean something more and more complex as the infant grows. [pp. 238–239]

I have found, in the analytic study of nearly three hundred pre-oedipal homosexual patients, and in a dozen or so sexual deviants, whether masochists, fetishists, transvestites, or transsexuals, that despite the various environments of each family, specific distorting influences could be isolated, influences that lead to emotional and cognitive difficulties characteristic of pre-oedipal perversion. I invariably found, for example, in my homosexual patients and others, an interlocking family pathology dating back to the patient's early years of life, affecting the child's separation–individuation process, profoundly interfering with his capacity to resolve his primary feminine identification, and producing severe ego deficiencies. The specific homosexogenic factor in the great majority of these families was a dominant mother in the area of child-rearing and influence, far from Winnicott's notion of the good-enough mother.

Indeed, the fault was not only the mother's, but the father's as well, for in these families the father has resigned power, authority, and rightfully held influence in the homosexogenic family through an "abdication" (Socarides, 1982). Paternal abdication, when it occurs in the context of a psychologically crushing mother, has especially severe consequences, for it makes the task of separation from the mother extremely difficult and leaves the child structurally deficient and developmentally arrested.

Of importance in homosexuals as well as in other perversions such as sadomasochism, transvestism, and voyeurism, there is almost always found a family situation in which there is no respect for the father, and this is communicated to the child from the very beginning of life (cf. Greenacre, 1968). I noted elsewhere (Socarides, 1982) that the father's libidinal and aggressive availability is a major requirement for the development of appropriate gender identity of all pre-homosexual children, as well as for those who develop other perversions. Such a father is not available as a love object for the child, nor is he available to the mother as a source of emotional support. If physically present, he rarely sets limits or prohibitions, but is often explicitly passive (Prall, 1978).

Examination of the infancy and childhood environment reveals a complete lack of facilitation towards integration. Many mothers of homosexuals, for example, suffer from a sense of low self-esteem and from castration anxiety and penis envy. These attitudes and fears profoundly influence their approach to their young male children. They may regard their sons' bodies as penis substitutes or as symbols of their own masculinity (cf. Mahler et al., 1975). They commonly treat their sons' bodies as if they were a part of themselves, or put obstacles in the way of their children's individuation and self-expression, especially during the quasi-negativistic phase beginning at the age of 2 years. Behaving contemptuously towards the phallic masculinity of their sons, they interfere with the formation of self-identity, as well as that of sexual identity, by crippling phallic self-assertion and self-esteem. The abdicating fathers do not interfere with the crushing attitudes of these mothers, for unless the father shows his readiness to be identified with, and the mother respects the father's masculinity and permits him to act as a role-model, the little boy is unable to dis-identify from the mother and establish an identification with the father (Greenson, 1968). This shift requires a mutual coopera- tion of mother, father, and child and, in Abelin's (1971) words, may well be "impossible for either [the mother or the child] to master without their having the father to turn to" (p. 248).

As the child proceeds into the rapprochement sub-phase of separation–individuation, he uses the mother to fulfil regressive fantasies, but the mother simultaneously arouses intense feelings of resentment and frustration. In contrast, the father, although taken for granted, may represent "a stable island of external re- ality, carrying over his role from the lost practicing paradise" (Abelin, 1971, p. 243). This is because there is less discrepancy between the child's image of the father and the real father at this age. During this period, when toddlers are disappointed by their mothers, they begin to evoke their fathers in their play, through drawings, calling them on the telephone or playing games with them, and by other methods of spontaneous father-play.

Such play is almost completely lacking in the history of pre- homosexual boys as well as in others who develop perversions, as reconstructed during their adult psychoanalysis or elicited from histories obtained from their families. Furthermore, it is strikingly apparent that pre-perverse children have great difficulty in attach- ing themselves to father substitutes as compared to normal children, who easily substitute older brothers, grandfathers, and other males for the father.

Thus, the pre-perverse child, brought up in a non-facilitating environment, cannot successfully negotiate his maturational phases of separation–individuation, which must be completed by the age of 3 years. The child's unconscious hostility reinforces de- nial of any of the mother's loving and giving aspects. He seeks to rediscover in his object choice—in the most distorted ways—his narcissistic relationship with the different images of the mother, and later of the father, as they were first experienced. Homosexu- ality, for example, can therefore be seen as an attempt to separate from the mother, from her engulfment due to an earlier inadequate intrapsychic separation, by running away from all women. Of central significance is the fact that the male sexual partner represents the father to whom the son is looking for salvation from engulfment. He is seeking a re-duplication of himself through the sexual act, for the object relationship is from object to self, whereby the self is represented by the homosexual partner.

There are two specific consequences that I have found in this family matrix: (1) the boundary between self and object, the self and mother, is blurred or incomplete, with a resultant persistence of primary feminine identification, and a disturbance in gender-defined self-identity; (2) this developmental deficiency produces an object relations type of conflict (Kernberg, 1975), one in which the patient experiences anxiety and guilt associated with the failure of development in the phase of self-object differentiation (Dorpat, 1976). The nuclear conflict of pre-oedipal perverts consists of a desire for and a dread of merging with the mother in order to reinstate the primitive mother–child unity with its associated separation anxiety or, if the fixation occurred during the practising or differentiating sub-phases, fragmentation anxiety due to a more severe and inadequate separation from the mother (Socarides, 1988).

I have found that there are dramatic re-enactments of rapprochement sub-phase crises secondary to attempts at intrapsychic separation from the mother during the treatment of perverse individuals (Socarides, 1980). These patients feel threatened, as they regress, with fear of maternal re-engulfment. Regressive experiences of this type are also a reflection of the father's earlier failure to function as one of a wide range of non-maternal objects helping the child to establish and to hold on to reality. For it is the father's love that helps diminish the child's fear of loss of the mother's love and loss of the object, a fear that can become so intense that the child's development spurt is completely blocked or frustrated, his reality function disturbed, and his integration damaged. If the child does not have the father to turn to, he experiences a severe deflation of his developing sense of self-esteem or his normal narcissism, caused by overwhelming feelings of weakness and painful realizations of his own helplessness. A self that has been rendered helpless and fragile by such developmental interferences is likely to develop extreme narcissistic vulnerability. A spurious sense of self-cohesion and self-esteem is then maintained by the construction of a pathological grandiose self (Kohut, 1971), which is a false self. As a result, narcissistic personality disorders are commonly found in association with perversions.

A normal boy must find his own identity as a prerequisite to the onset of both true object relations and partial identification with his parents. To the male homosexual, for example, I have found in infancy that, on the one hand, the mother had been dangerous and frightening, forcing separation, and threatening the infant with loss of love; on the other hand, the mother's conscious and unconscious tendencies are felt as working against separation. Anxiety and frustration press for withdrawal of libido from the mother and an increase in aggression. The resulting introjected bad mother imago leads to a split in the ego in order to maintain the image of the good mother. In his narcissistic object choice, the homosexual, for example, not only loves his partner as he himself wished to be loved by the mother, but also reacts to him with the sadistic aggression that he once experienced towards the hostile mother for forcing separation.

Stoller (1975b) has also carefully described what amounts to a facilitating environment which produces normal children in which the gesture is congruent with the child's needs. In such an environment, the parents must have an unequivocal conviction that the infant is a biologically normal male, and they confirm this by the sensations that he experiences from his genitals, as well as seeing them. Even though the infant is not immediately aware of his particular genitals, this must be part of the unquestioned acceptance of him and his anatomy as a male by the parents. Also, there must be an encouragement of phase-adequate separation from mother's body, with mother not only feeling but also expressing her pleasure at the infant's capacity to separate from her body. Furthermore, there must be an acceptance of this individuation— that is, the development of the knowledge that one is a unique individual with precise, definable, valuable, and permanent attributes.

The mother and father must feel and express pleasure at the infant's capacity in becoming a distinct individual. The mother must encourage the boy, at the appropriate time, to do masculine things. Masculinity can be defined for the child by expression of attitudes that the mother has learned from society, and from her own style in interpreting these attitudes. In addition, her capacity to accept masculinity in males, and her relatively unambivalent pleasure in the boy's maleness, are all important. Encouragement by the father is increasingly helpful as the child separates from his mother. A father must be present physically and psychologically and serve as a model for identification. He must also act as a shield to protect his son if the boy's mother has any reflex anti-masculinity that she unthinkingly directs at her son for being male (Stoller, 1975b). The enjoyment of her husband's masculinity makes it easier for the boy to identify with his father. A reinforcement of the sense of identity will take place by seduction from the mother, according to Stoller, which makes it clear that he is an external object clearly differentiated from her body and psyche, an object that she wants to possess again, but at this time not as a content of her womb but as a "male with his own identity" (Stoller, 1975b, p. 240). All these parental influences play an essential part in producing a facilitating environment and in promoting maturation.

### Symptomatology arising from maturational disturbances

Certain symptoms arise from the faulty gender identity:

1.  There is a continuation of the persistence of the primary feminine identification with the mother, resulting in inner feelings of femininity which may be somewhat conscious, but largely unconscious.

2.  There is also a corresponding feeling of a deficit in masculinity, with anxiety appearing when faced with attempted performance in the appropriate anatomical gender role.

3.  Furthermore, one finds an intense oral-sadistic relationship with the mother, intense sadism towards her disguised by its opposite—namely, a masochistic attitude towards her—with passive homosexual feelings towards the father, often re-

pressed, as well as the wish to wreak vengeance on the father through appropriating his penis. The latter all arise from the wish for, and the fear of, extreme closeness to the mother, and an intense dependency on her for a feeling of well-being and a sense of survival.

4.    Additionally, there is often a fear of the sudden approach from the mother and other women, as if they could devour, engulf, and incorporate the man. This fear of the mother's engulfment and control reflects in part the wish for and the dread of her domination, which is then generalized to a fear of all women, of engulfment by them, especially by the female genitalia and pubic hair.

5.    At puberty, hormonal stimulation and anatomic growth lead to an intensification of anxiety due to the deficient masculine identity, and an inability to perform in the masculine, anatomical, physiological, and psychological role. The result is powerful feelings of anxiety, shame, and guilt, as well as hostility towards one's penis and masculinity, which reinforce aspects of the feminine identification such as mood, manner, stance, posture, dress, voice, facial expression, hand gestures, areas of interest, and so forth.

6.    Sensing a defect in masculinity, homosexuals may then engage in compensatory masculinization or further false-self integration through weightlifting, body-building, and heightened narcissistic overevaluation of their own body.

7.    An insistent and imperative need for same-sex gratification and incorporation of the male penis in identification with a male homosexual partner begins to make its appearance.

### The infantile genetic matrix of depression and perversion

Winnicott deserves a special position among those who have studied the depressive affect and its importance for child development, and its role in later psychopathology. Notable among these analytical authors have been Jacobson (1946), Bibring (1953), Spitz (1959), and Mahler (1966). More recently, Socarides and Stolorow (1985), strongly influenced by Winnicott's ideas and by Kohutian concepts, concluded that all depressive disorders have their origin in "early selfobject failure, leading to an inability to integrate depressive feelings" (p. 113). They asserted:

> The depressive affect is integrated into the structure of the self through consistent, reliable, empathic selfobject attunements. ... The capacity to identify and withstand depressive feelings without a corresponding loss of self, fear of self dissolution, or a tendency to somatize the affect has its origin in the early affect-relatedness between the child and primary care giver. [p. 113]

The authors go on to confirm Winnicott's earlier observations, noting that what is crucial to the child's development is

> his growing capacity to integrate his sadness and his painful disappointments in himself and others—the reliable presence of a calming, containing, empathic selfobject, irrespective of the "amount" or intensity of the affects involved. [p. 114]

Furthermore, I have found consistently that perverse acts function to reduce suffering due both to anxiety and to the painful affect of depression. The relief of the depressive affect through perverse acts helps to restore the self against threats of fragmentation, diminishes separation anxiety, and compensates for narcissistic injuries. It constitutes an eroticized flight from despair and help-lessness, perceived in the unconscious as a threat of starvation, a finding common in depressed patients. Through eroticization, the pervert attempts to diminish or erase anxiety and depression (Bibring, 1953), as well as lessen the anxiety arising from crumbling, fragmenting, and disintegrating self and object representations. Through acting out, an intrapsychic crisis is diverted into perverse acts; there is also a denial of sensation of depression, heaviness, and sadness despite specifically opposite sensations (Socarides, 1985, 1988).

It is tempting to note here that the word "gay", commonly and currently used to denote homosexuals and homosexuality, with its connotation of liveliness, gladness, joy, and merriment, represents a wholesale flight from the opposite sensations—namely, sadness, misery, and despair (Socarides, 1985). These emotions are a defensive position against the depressive aspects arising from the failure of maternal holding. They enable an individual to escape the deadness of an internal world, the futility and ego depletion secondary to the inability to establish sustained and permanent object relations.

Always the keen observer, Winnicott (1935) noted that a denial of certain aspects of depression may be facilitated through symbols. Bright clothing or articles such as diaphragms, douche accompaniments, and so on have both depressive and contra-depressive significance. A young, cherubic, prepubertal youth, or a youthful adolescent of a particular type, he noted, may function for a paedophile or for an ageing homosexual as a contra-depressant equivalent. The use of colourful clothing or a humorous mode may perpetuate a defensive position against the depressive affect.

### Concluding comments

I shall finish this all too brief review and appreciation of some of Winnicott's contributions to the understanding of the origin and the matrix of sexual perversion by citing one of his earlier papers, "Aggression in Relation to Emotional Development" (Winnicott, 1950a). One observes in this paper Winnicott's scientific method of working, applying his keen observational and creative powers to the study of the relationship between environmental impingement of motility in the earliest years of life to the later development of sadistic and masochistic trends in adults. As he wrote, "Where there is environmental impingement, there is ill-health", for impingement leads "to non-fusion of the aggression and libido" (p. 212), which is then expressed in a secondary fashion through eroticization of the aggression.

In a creative leap, Winnicott made a truly valuable suggestion:

Here is the root for compulsive sadistic trends [that are] destructive and ruthless. He [the perverse individual] tries to bring about relationships through interplay with another individual by finding an erotic component to fuse with the aggression which is not in itself much more than pure motility. Here the erotic achieves fusion with motility, whereas in health it is more true to say that motility fuses with the erotic. . . . It is probable that in the perversions two kinds of masochism can be distinguished; one kind comes from a sadism which is an eroticization of a true motility urge, and the other kind is a more direct eroticization of the passive or active motility; and it would appear that the development is directed one way or the other according to whether the first partner was masochistic or sadistic. The partnership produces a relationship which is valued but more because relationships were feeble when developed out of the erotic life, owing to a relative lack of fusion of motility elements into the erotic life. [p. 213]

# CHAPTER TEN

# On the capacity for being inside enough

*Murray Cox*

Most patients in Broadmoor Hospital are legally detained "without limit of time", so that the phrase "being inside enough" could carry an ironic connotation. It can also refer to the depths of the personality reached during prolonged forensic psychotherapy. Furthermore, the therapist's auto-audit constantly questions whether the patient's defensive organization, which precipitated the "criminal act", has been adequately relinquished. In other words, in that complex mutuality between therapist and patient, which is a *sine qua non* of effective psychotherapy, the question hovering over both therapist and patient has to do with their reciprocal "capacity for being inside enough". Such modified mutuality—which is partial, reversible, and at the therapist's discretion—is exemplified in the simplicity of the squiggle that the psychotherapist starts and then invites the patient to continue.

Donald Winnicott's influence is so pervasive and powerful that he is an ever-present prompter to those attempting to write about dynamic psychotherapy. Even within the relatively circumscribed field of adult forensic psychotherapy, with which he had some direct contact as a paediatrician and as a psychoanalyst, phrases of his are constantly at the ready, as we shall shortly see. Having an interest in those metaphors that change things—*mutative metaphors* (Cox & Theilgaard, 1987)—it seems appropriate to launch these reflections with Goldman's words:

> The growing interest in Winnicott is also the result of the powerful metaphors he fashioned, such as holding environment, good-enough mother, transitional object, and True and False Self. Winnicott's ideas were rarely expressed as exact logical concepts; rather, they were in Guntrip's (1975, p. 155) words, "imaginative hypotheses that challenged one to explore further". Metaphors are a form of symbolization that bridges the known and the unknown, the conscious and unconscious, the personal and the universal. The imaginative act of metaphor making is one of the ways in which we construct reality (Siegelman, 1990). [Goldman, 1993, p. xiii]

Interestingly, during a group therapy session conducted only minutes before this chapter was posted to the editor, a psychotic patient said, "I've lost my character. I've lost my true self!"

This chapter explores the relevance of some aspects of these "powerful metaphors" that are of such direct impact within the broad sweep of forensic psychotherapy itself, though there is an added cachet about their more focused significance when viewed from the particular vantage point of psychotherapy undertaken in a secure setting. Winnicott was "present", and it seemed to matter little whether I was writing a review article on the "holding function" of dynamic psychotherapy in a custodial setting (Cox, 1986) or trying to convey the *ethos* of forensic psychotherapy in an appendix to a book describing the performance of tragedy in a secure psychiatric hospital (Cox, 1992). In the first instance, there was a direct quotation from Winnicott, whereas in the second the significance of inter-generational playing was an allusive aura rather than a direct quotation. This dual mode of stimulus seems to me to be characteristic of Winnicott's different kinds of impingement upon the presentation of the psychotherapeutic process.

I am aware of an almost suffocating requirement for condensation at this point. Because of my twenty-five years experience as a psychotherapist in a secure hospital, treating aggressive psychopaths and homicidal psychotics, this means that I have spent years in the company of those who so often seem to have reached the point of almost knowing themselves utterly. Forensic therapeutic space testifies to the fact that serious playfulness can be virtually irresistible. Indeed, if I was asked to write on one—and only one— aspect of Winnicott's contributions to forensic psychotherapy undertaken with the most serious offender-patients of all, I would choose to write on the capacity to play, and to play safely. This depends upon gradually developing reciprocal trust and the nature of that which not only safely holds both patient and psychotherapist, but also holds them together. This, in turn, will depend upon "their capacity for being inside enough". This amalgam of themes refers not only to being "inside"—using the slang for a custodial sentence—but also, through reciprocal projective identification, to being inside each other enough to trust the more threatening possibility of actually entering oneself, enough. Of immense significance at this point is the nature of the wall that contains, encloses, and renders safe. This concept of *murality* can receive no more than passing mention here, though it is a primary dynamic, forensic consideration (Cox & Theilgaard, 1994). Having now reached the theme of "on the capacity for being inside enough", we shall look further at the part played by playing within forensic therapeutic space.

References to being inside, and to being "inside enough", often carry implicit or explicit sexual connotations, sometimes both. Thus, forced penetrative "inside enoughness" is one of the forensic features of rape, whereas satisfied lovers will refer to being deeply inside each other's bodies, minds, and lives. Drama is steeped in oblique references to sexual access—the possibility of being "inside enough" and the blocks thereto. For example, Lear speaking to Regan says [*King Lear*, II.iv.175]:

> 'Tis not in thee
> . . . to oppose the bolt
> Against my coming in.

The play is rich in multiple meanings and ambiguities, pointing towards a massive failure of transgenerational inside-enoughness. So much so that imagination almost fails at the thought of the King

Lear *dramatis personae*, one by one, tying and untying communication links when playing with string or inheriting an unfinished squiggle. How would Goneril's differ from Regan's?

There is always a danger that the use of technical terms may convey an impression of spurious precision. That is why this chapter refers to the importance of playing with ideas, without trying to define too closely what the process of playing actually is. The thematic groundswell, beneath surface ripples and tidal rhythms, has to do with the spontaneity and fun of playfulness in the inherently serious dynamic issues lying at the core of forensic psychotherapy.

So great is Winnicott's impact as a writer that he almost occludes the recall of others who have written on the same subject. For example, if one is playing the serious brainstorming game of linking themes and authors and is offered the stimulus word "Play"—there is usually a silent period of stalling after "Winnicott" has been blurted out, almost before the "question mark" had been reached. Huizinga, who wrote *Homo Ludens* (1949), a major work with a far wider frame of reference, tends to follow after a considerable latent period, if he follows at all. Yet *Homo Ludens* and Reality is, surely, Winnicott Man in a Facilitating Environment.

In order to attain a reasonable degree of focus within the confines of a chapter, the twin themes of Winnicott and forensic psychotherapy are looked at here from a third triangulation point. Borrowing the technique of the surveyor and the navigator, our thematic location will be determined by taking bearings from the fixed point of play. But can there be a fixed point of playfulness, which implies capricious, uncertain instabilities? "Now expectation . . . sets all on hazard" (*Troilus and Cressida*, Prologue: 20) and the play, like many clinical histories, starts where the patient "is", by "beginning in the middle". Even so, this playful distancing and affirmation of framing points of reference have now given a setting sufficiently well defined to enclose the title of these deliberations: "on the capacity for being inside enough"—with its triple, one might say triangular, Winnicottian allusive energy. Depending on the reader's perspectival point of engagement with Winnicott, one of three possible allusive bells will be set ringing by this composite title. First, there is "The Capacity to Be Alone" (Winnicott, 1958b), secondly, there is his sentence that contains the trigger word "enough", to wit, "mothers who have it in them to provide good enough care" (Winnicott, 1960b, p. 591). Thirdly, though not by Winnicott himself, come the words of Grolnick (1990) who referred to him as "master of the middle, the in-between" who "turned compromise and conflict into paradox, paradox that dances between polarities" (p. 3). The linked themes implicit in the title of this chapter point to the fabric of this contribution, which has been so woven that a pattern gradually emerges in which Winnicott's crucial relevance to forensic issues will be indisputable. Furthermore, a personal essay of this nature can only be written from the perspectival world of the author. Although emphasis is placed upon Winnicott's associative playfulness, there are other equally important forensic impingements, in terms of theory and technique.

I have always sensed an implicit welcome somehow invisibly evident between the lines when reading Winnicott. I first described this in 1978 (Cox, 1978), and I feel it even more strongly today. This awareness of welcome stems, in part, from enthusiasms of an experienced practitioner in the "hands-on" field of paediatrics—which is so intimately linked to that of general practice. Reading Winnicott, one never detects a hint of the "keep out, you are not trained" ethos that can colour some jealously guarded professional territories. On the contrary, one can almost overhear him saying, "Come in. This is so interesting. I, myself, don't fully understand it. I wonder if we can un-baffle it a little, together?"

We are now engaging with the theme "on being inside enough", and we do so indirectly as Winnicott, himself, might have done. As an ally we may invoke Shakespeare's help and "by indirections find direction out" (*Hamlet*, II.i.64)—the only problem being that one can find support in Shakespeare for virtually every approach to everything! Therefore, to be more specific, words by States (1978) encourage us: "Pockets of emptiness are never reliably insignificant" (p. 31). Are we not closer to Winnicott when we say that this is of the essence of the squiggle approach? There are echoes of the projective games that Hamlet and Polonius played on clouds, which Rorschach (1921) played on ink blots, and Cox and Theilgaard (1987, p. 26) link to the creative energy within the aesthetic imperative which "finds directions out" in the course of dynamic psychotherapy. When considering a "major", say, homicidal, forensic history, the initially apparently trivial detail may ultimately assume significance of pivotal proportions, such that States's dictum could be reshaped: "Pockets of apparent emptiness are often reliably significant." Projective questioning plays a prominent part in forensic assessments, as is evident in the invaluable "Peter Scott Question"—"Looking back on it all now, how do you feel about it?" The patient declares much about his inner world by the presumed implicit referent "on it all". Does it refer to, say, the index offence, a court appearance, or childhood abuse or to the first realization of being a Broadmoor patient? Such indirect projective questioning plays a crucial part in forensic interviewing and is so often in counterpoint to the unavoidable impact of the direct question: "Was the knife in your hand when she came into the room?"

This Winnicott-seeking enterprise is now at the place of play in the theatre—"the play's the thing, wherein . . . " many forensic thematic threads will be caught. There is an inherent paradox in the relationship between live theatre and the closely related—though highly different—media of film and television. It can be succinctly stated as follows: whereas, by definition, the former takes place in the presence of a live audience, the latter does not. Nevertheless, the playfulness of the play is most itself during the rehearsal process, in which mistakes are made, experiment and trial-and-error is the rule, but where, again virtually by definition, there is no live audience! There are many similarities here to various matching frames within the world of therapy. Some of these have been studied in *Shakespeare as Prompter: The Amending Imagination and the Therapeutic Process* (Cox & Theilgaard, 1994). But there are additional aspects that are relevant at this point. For example, all the spontaneity, fun, and laughter that so often feature in living therapy somehow strangely wilt when reported "secondhand" to a supervisor. The humour, which sometimes prompts all those within therapeutic space to enjoy a playful phase, seems arid and tedious when reported in a subsequent seminar on the therapeutic process. This leads us to an interesting alternative, scenic route as part of our journey, which, because of thematic and spatial constraints, can only be mentioned as being worth exploring. I refer to the linking of the topics of playfulness and privacy. As Winnicott (1965) himself writes, "In poetry, something true crystallizes out; to plan our lives we need science" (p. 173). In his posthumously published paper entitled "Fear of Breakdown" (1974), Winnicott writes, "Naturally, if what I say has truth in it, this will already have been dealt with by the world's poets, but the flashes of insight that come in poetry cannot absolve us from our painful task of getting step by step away from ignorance towards our goal" (p. 103).

Winnicott's juxtaposition of the phrases "flashes of insight" and "step by step" progress in the passage just quoted is congruous with the phenomenon of aesthetic access to the personality (Cox & Theilgaard, 1994). One of the goals of forensic psychotherapy is the establishment of contact with empathy-resistant patients, who usually present as narcissistic personality disorders or as fragile disintegrating psychotics. I cannot overemphasize the paramount importance of defence-bypassing, aesthetic access to the personality of the hitherto empathy-resistant patient.

It would be relatively easy to describe conventional clusters of forensic psychopathology, often leading to particular shapings of the criminal act, and to delineate Winnicott's contribution to early aberrations of the developmental line which, subsequently, led to a life history of "forensic proportions" (Cox, 1990, p. 632). Nevertheless, considering Winnicott's forensic contribution from such an angle, though it would be of value within the covers of a textbook, would miss the dynamic at the heart of the matter—namely, playing. *Playing and Reality* (Winnicott, 1971) must be one of the best-known publications in both professional circles and serious popular reading. Yet the capacity to play, to experiment, to reorganize, and to reframe material is inherent in both science and art, therapy and theology, living and loving—so that man needs to be *homo ludens* if he is to be fully himself. Winnicott (1967, p. 368) asks, "where is play?" in his essay "The Location of Cultural Experience", and he goes on to answer his own question:

> when we witness an infant's employment of a transitional object, the first not-me possession, we are witnessing both the child's first use of a symbol and the first experience of play. [p. 369]

With unavoidably ironic precision, Phillips (1993) ends his paper in *Winnicott Studies Vol. 8*, entitled "Contingency for Beginners", with this sentence: "We are all beginners at contingency because it is the only thing to be" (p. 45). This reminds me of an advertisement for a dancing school which invited potential participants to join one of the following classes: "Absolute, Intermediate, and Advanced Beginners!" There is something inherently Winnicottian about this invitation. Indeed, the possibility of ever outgrowing the capacity to play invites the prospect of a rusty fossil scarcely able to creak from chair to couch, undoubtedly incapable of enjoying the catalytic crucible where cultural experience renews itself. One hopes to retain the inquisitiveness of the Absolute Beginner until the Absolute End and the *Exeunt All*.

One of the privileges of forensic psychotherapy undertaken with patients in a setting where it is possible to explore the inner world without limit of time is the never-ending possibility of possibility itself. Kierkegaard, a great comfort to forensic psychotherapists and their patients, defined hope as "a passion for the possible" in contrast to wishful thinking of the impossible. In the perceptual set of this author at least, the beginning of any therapy session, no matter whether it is conducted within individual or group therapeutic space, has something about it of the playful possibility that almost anything could happen. The therapeutic skill is to let this dawning realization take place *safely*, and the inherent momentum of the mutative metaphor ensures this. Often the peculiar *gravitas* of forensic psychotherapy is evident at the phase when protective illusions fail, and the offence, say rape, comes to be seen as a self-esteem regulator for a psychologically impotent man, whose fragility precludes warmth and intimacy. The sheer phenomenology of that which is about to be presented to the attention of the theatre audience, at the moment when the curtain rises, has many parallels in therapeutic space. The process of *poiesis* takes over as the session begins. Paradoxically enough, it is just as active and exciting (in an etymological and maybe even a popular sense) in the one hundred and fiftieth session as it is in the first. There is always that which is about to be called into existence which was not there before (*poiesis*)—and this may take the form of some new reordering of the kaleidoscopic pattern of transference and countertransference energies. It may take the form of fresh understanding of a relationship in childhood, and this is often linked to a fresh appraisal of the dynamics of the "index offence" —to use Special Hospital vernacular.

If we were looking for forensic anchor-points in Winnicott's work, we should make the obvious point that Winnicott was dealing primarily with early life experience and with disturbed children, which explains the absence of adult forensic psychotherapy until relatively recently. It is for this reason that it is no surprise to see that Special Hospitals do not feature in the index of his book *Deprivation and Delinquency* (Winnicott, 1984). Nevertheless, he knew about the vital importance of a containing environment, which brings us to the axiomatic and pivotal Winnicottian theme of the facilitating environment and its link with the holding environment (Cox, 1986).

Winnicott (1961a) comments on environments and experience from which a disturbed child runs away. It is one of the early professional benchmarks in forensic psychotherapy to note the complex interrelationship of the process of running and whether the motivation is primarily running away *from* or running *to*. There are echoes here of the personal uniqueness of running styles—we can all recognize John by the way he jogs, even when seen across the park. The ancient reference (Samuel, 18:22–27) to this is: "when a man is running alone there are tidings on his tongue. . . . Behold I see another man running alone and his running is like the running of Ahimaaz." Winnicott (1961a, p. 207) also refers to the "absconder on his return", and there are many activated prodigal associations. Winnicott rightly constantly stresses the importance of detail. One man running alone is not to be mistaken for another solitary runner.

If we are to pick up the "dancing with Donald" theme, we could do so through the forensic citations that are linked to the playful, dancing quality of the *aesthetic imperative* (Cox & Theilgaard, 1987, 1994), which perhaps takes us into the other dance. In *The Universal Drum*, Rodgers (1979) writes, "But we are not destroyed . . . and we follow the poet [William Carlos Williams] who flings himself "into the other dance, to the other music" (p. 182).

We are again caught by Winnicott's sense of serious playfulness, with all the subtextual implications that erupt in consideration of forensic psychotherapy. There is the suggestion that we might justly worry if we felt we had progressed beyond the stage of being "an advanced beginner". Like the applicants for the dancing school, we could join the class as beginners, intermediate, or even advanced beginners! Winnicott has a way of cutting us down to size. Playfulness rebukes those who feel that, in understanding the privacy of the inner world of another, they might have surpassed their peers and moved beyond the stage of being, at best, an advanced beginner!

But why "dancing with Donald"? Not only because Grolnick (1990, p. 3) links the name of Winnicott with "paradox that dances between . . . polarities", but because the *poiesis* that energizes all creative writing evokes echoes of "dancing like Dolphins"—a phrase borrowed from *Antony and Cleopatra* (V.ii.89):

> His delights
> were dolphin-like: they show'd his back above
> The element they lived in.

The very playfulness, the unpredictable up-and-downness of the dolphin splashing into and out of the unconscious, is the recollection of Brockbank's observation that "Shakespeare uses a polarizing lens that brings the colours out" (quoted in Cox & Theilgaard, 1994, n.p.). Here, Cleopatra plays with the image of dolphins jumping out of one element before they return and plunge deeper into other depths. This is part of the perpetual polarity of playfulness which is both predictably unpredictable, safely risky, and repeatedly novel. Novelty is of the essence of much that Winnicott stands for. It is also an intrinsic part of successful forensic psychotherapy. This is because the hardened narcissistic personality, often presenting phenomenologically as an aggressive psychopath, is unable to habituate to that which is novel. It explains why the aesthetic imperative is so well endowed in reaching the inner world of the heavily defended brittle patient, who, in defence, has developed a carapace of steel-like resistance. The playfulness of the squiggle and the paradoxically successful invasiveness of the aesthetic imperative, which does not invade, is evident here. To quote Gaston Bachelard (1969, p. xix), "But the image has touched the depths before it stirs the surface". Much of the playful component of forensic psychotherapy was foreshadowed by Winnicott's early work in successfully approaching disturbed children, who were afraid to be approached. This is because such an indirect approach does not enter the world of the other from without. On the contrary, there is a growing realization within the individual himself that something is changing shape and assuming energy, and the psychotherapist is alongside him as he tries to answer his own tacit self-question: "What might these things—these feelings—be?" When originally planning this chapter, one possible title that presented itself was "play's the thing". This phrasing with irresistible allusions from Hamlet could stand as a "one-liner" on Winnicott's forensic contributions. Indeed, if there were to be a sudden drastic reduction in the publication budget of this volume and each contributor was asked to reduce what he had written to three words, mine would be PLAY'S THE THING. This would stand as a reasonable compression of a statement embracing Winnicott's contribution to forensic psychotherapy.

"Play's the thing" brings us to the stable quicksands of the squiggle—the precarious security of being alone in the presence of another, the good-enough carer, the threateningly protective, the demanding support, the supportive confrontation—indeed, those paradoxes, and the oxymoron, have the stamp of Donald Winnicott upon them. Instead of pursuing a traditional presentation and the vignettes of Winnicott-witnessing quotations, this chapter has relocated such themes upon a broader canvas.

Playfulness, the squiggle, and the aesthetic imperative return us to the Winnicottian paradigm of "The Capacity for Being Inside Enough". The ubiquitous man in the street when asked how long he has been inside tends to answer this question in terms of the presence or absence of a criminal record, rather than the time spent indoors, as opposed to time spent in the garden. But the adequacy of intrauterine nourishment and growth, so that neither too little nor too much time was spent within the mother before cascading into the outside world and the initiation of other modes of being the primary maternal preoccupation, is never far from Winnicottian considerations. It is also close to core determining factors of forensic psychopathology. One generic Broadmoor Hospital anecdote must suffice. During a group therapy session, the constantly recurring theme of mothers and mothering came to the surface:

"Don't mention mothers to me", barked Dave, a relative new-
comer. . . . When I was a young kid, mum said she was going
down the road for a loaf of bread and THE BUGGER NEVER
CAME BACK."

The ensuing sessions, the unfolding life story, the escalating forensic enactments and increasing seriousness of the subsequent
criminal acts were all explicable in terms of the sequential failures
of mother substitutes. Authority figures were tested and goaded
until they could not help proving unreliable, which therefore reca-
pitulated the primary maternal abandonment. It was only after
much testing and testing-out, acting and acting-out, that Dave's
assessment of life finally came down in favour of trusting those
who were initially presumed not to be reliable, precisely because
they were in positions of trust. Furthermore, as with all forensic
histories, we do not yet know the end of the story. All we know
for sure is that death is "the impassable frontier . . . before which
are called to a halt"—to quote Barth's (1928, p. 168) magisterial
words.

In summary, it can be claimed that the capacity to be inside
enough, within the therapeutic relationship, within a secure setting, is intimately linked to the patient's capacity to trust. There is
an inherent paradox and mystery at the heart of these things—
because the more that hitherto trustworthy relationships have
proved to fail, the more must the capacity to trust and be trustworthy be taken on trust. This will depend upon the early life experiences, the "inside enoughness", of the therapist himself or herself
and his or her subsequent capacity to discriminate between things
that are internal and internalized, external and externalized.

Playing is a serious business. Winnicott has given a priceless
lead to sombre forensic issues when the ideational and affective
homologue—via the aesthetic imperative—can lead to the safe
understanding of the inner world of even the most disturbed
offender-patient. Blasphemous though it may be, these deliberations could end with the couplet,

"The play's the thing,
Wherein the psyche's understood through string!"

There is something here about the intermittent, tidal capacity to be inside each other enough, which is of the essence of therapy. It can only take place as mutual trust grows and begins to unfold its wings. It may be a prelude to both Intimacy and Ultimacy, which must remain the *ne plus ultra* of experience.

# REFERENCES

Abelin, E. L. (1971). The role of the father in the separation–individuation process. In: J. B. McDevitt & C. F. Settlage (Eds.), *Separation-Individuation: Essays in Honor of Margaret S. Mahler* (pp. 229–252). New York: International Universities Press.

Bachelard, G. (1969). *The Poetics of Space*. Boston, MA: Beacon Press.

Barth, K. (1928). *The Word of God and the Word of Man*, trans. D. Horton. London: Hodder & Stoughton.

Beebe, B., & Lachmann, F. (1988). Mother–infant mutual influence and precursors of psychic structure. In: A. Goldberg (Ed.), *Progress in Self Psychology, Vol. 3: Frontiers in Self Psychology* (pp. 3–25). Hillsdale, NJ: Analytic Press.

Bibring, E. (1953). The mechanism of depression. In: P. Greenacre (Ed.), *Affective Disorders: Psychoanalytic Contribution to Their Study* (pp. 13–48). New York: International Universities Press.

Boris, H. M. (1984). The problem of anorexia nervosa. *International Journal of Psycho-Analysis*, 65: 315–322.

Bowlby, J., Miller, E., & Winnicott, D. W. (1939). Evacuation of small children. *British Medical Journal* (16 December): 1202–1203.

Braten, S. (1987). Dialogic mind: the infant and the adult in proto conversation. In: M. Carvallo (Ed.), *Nature, Cognition and Systems* (pp. 187–205). Dordrecht: D. Reidel.

Brazelton, T. B., Koslowski, B., & Main, M. (1974). The origins of reciprocity: the early mother–infant interaction. In: M. Lewis & L. Rosenblum (Eds.), *The Effect of the Infant on its Caregiver* (pp. 49–76). New York: John Wiley.

Cox, M. (1978). *Structuring Therapeutic Process: Compromise with Chaos. The Therapist's Response to the Individual and the Group.* Oxford: Pergamon Press.

Cox, M. (1986). The "holding function" of dynamic psychotherapy in a custodial setting: a review. *Journal of the Royal Society of Medicine*, 79: 162–164.

Cox, M. (1990). Psychopathology and treatment of psychotic aggression. In: R. Bluglass & P. Bowden (Eds.), *Principles and Practice of Forensic Psychiatry* (pp. 631–639). Edinburgh: Churchill Livingstone.

Cox, M. (1992). Forensic psychiatry and forensic psychotherapy. In: M. Cox (Ed.), *Shakespeare Comes to Broadmoor: "The Actors Are Come Hither". The Performance of Tragedy in a Secure Psychiatric Hospital* (pp. 253–258). London: Jessica Kingsley.

Cox, M., & Theilgaard, A. (1987). *Mutative Metaphors in Psychotherapy: The Aeolian Mode.* London: Tavistock Publications.

Cox, M., & Theilgaard, A. (1994). *Shakespeare as Prompter: The Amending Imagination and the Therapeutic Process.* London: Jessica Kingsley.

Cross, L. W. (1993). Body and self in feminine development: implications for eating disorders and delicate self-mutilation. *Bulletin of the Menninger Clinic*, 57: 41–63.

Deutsch, H. (1942). Some forms of emotional disturbances and their relationship to schizophrenia. *Psychoanalytic Quarterly*, 11: 301–321.

Dorpat, T. L. (1976). Structural conflict and object relations conflict. *Journal of the American Psychoanalytic Association*, 24: 855–875.

Eissler, K. R. (1961). A hitherto unnoticed letter by Sigmund Freud. *International Journal of Psycho-Analysis*, 42: 197–204.

Fairbairn, W. R. D. (1941). A revised psychopathology of the psychoses and psychoneuroses. *International Journal of Psycho-Analysis*, 22: 250–279.

Fraiberg, S. (1969). Libidinal object constancy and mental representation. *Psychoanalytic Study of the Child*, 24: 48–70.

Fraiberg, S., Adelson, E., & Shapiro, V. (1975). Ghosts in the nursery: a psychoanalytic approach to the problems of impaired infant–mother relationships. *Journal of the American Academy of Child Psychiatry*, 14: 387–421.

Freud, A. (1965). *Normality and Pathology in Childhood: Assessments of*

*Development*. London: Hogarth Press & The Institute of Psycho-Analysis.

Freud, S. (1894a). The neuro-psychoses of defence. *S.E.*, *3*, pp. 45–61.

Freud, S. (1896b). Further remarks on the neuro-psychoses of defence. *S.E.*, *3*, pp. 162–185.

Freud, S. (1900a). *The Interpretation of Dreams. S.E.*, *4–5*.

Freud, S. (1906b). Psycho-analysis and the establishement of the facts in legal proceedings. *S.E.*, *9*, pp. 103–114.

Freud, S. (1906c). My views on the part played by sexuality in the aetiology of the neuroses. *S.E.*, *7*, pp. 271–279.

Freud, S. (1910c). *Leonardo da Vinci and a Memory of His Childhood. S.E.*, *11*, pp. 63–137.

Freud, S. (1911b). Formulations on the two principles of mental functioning. *S.E.*, *12*, pp. 218–226.

Freud, S. (1911c [1910]). Psycho-analytic notes on an autobiographical account of a case of paranoia (Dementia paranoides). *S.E.*, *12*, pp. 9–79.

Freud, S. (1915c). Instincts and their vicissitudes. *S.E.*, *14*, pp. 117–140.

Freud, S. (1916d). Some character-types met with in psycho-analytic work. *S.E.*, *14*, pp. 311–333.

Freud, S. (1919e). A child is being beaten. *S.E.*, *17*, pp. 179–204.

Freud, S. (1920a). The psychogenesis of a case of homosexuality in a woman. *S.E.*, *18*, pp. 147–172.

Freud, S. (1924b [1923]). Neurosis and psychosis. *S.E.*, *19*, pp. 149–153.

Freud, S. (1924e). The loss of reality in neurosis and psychosis. *S.E.*, *19*, pp. 183–187.

Freud, S. (1925f). Preface to Aichhorn's *Wayward Youth. S.E.*, *19*, pp. 273–275.

Freud, S. (1927e). Fetishism. *S.E.*, *21*, pp. 149–158.

Freud, S. (1928b). Dostoevsky and parricide. *S.E.*, *21*, pp. 177–194.

Freud, S. (1930a). *Civilization and its Discontents. S.E.*, *21*, pp. 64–145.

Freud, S. (1931d). The expert opinion in the Halsmann case. *S.E.*, *21*, pp. 251–253.

Freud, S. (1932a). The acquisition and control of fire. *S.E.*, *22*, pp. 187–193.

Giovacchini, P. L. (1958). Mutual adaptations in various object relationships. *International Journal of Psycho-Analysis*, *39*, 1–8.

Giovacchini, P. L. (1964). The submerged ego. *Journal of the American Academy of Child Psychiatry*, *3*: 430–442.

Giovacchini, P. L. (1965). Treatment of marital disharmonies: the classical approach. In: B. Greene (Ed.), *The Psychotherapies of Marital Disharmony* (pp. 39–81). New York: Free Press.

Giovacchini, P. L. (1967). Characterological aspects of marital interaction. *Psychoanalytic Forum*, 2: 7–13.

Giovacchini, P. L. (1972). The blank self. In: P.L. Giovacchini (Ed.), *Tactics and Techniques in Psychoanalytic Therapy* (pp. 364–378). New York: Science House.

Giovacchini, P. L. (1993). *Borderline Patients: The Psychosomatic Focus and the Therapeutic Process*. Northvale, NJ: Jason Aronson.

Giovacchini, P. L. (2000). *Impact of Narcissism: The Errant Therapist on a Chaotic Quest*. Northvale, NJ: Jason Aronson.

Golding, W. (1980). *Darkness Visible*. London: Faber & Faber.

Goldman, D. (1993). *In Search of the Real: The Origins and Originality of D. W. Winnicott*. Northvale, NJ: Jason Aronson.

Granoff, W., & Perrier, F. (1980). *El Problema de la Perversión en la Mujer*. Barcelona: Editorial Crítica.

Greenacre, P. (1968). Perversions: general considerations regarding their genetic and dynamic background. *Psychoanalytic Study of the Child*, 23: 47–62.

Greenacre, P. (1969). The fetish and the transitional object. In: *Emotional Growth, Vol. 1* (pp. 315–334). New York: International Universities Press.

Greenson, R. (1968). Disidentifying from the mother: its special importance to the boy. *International Journal of Psycho-Analysis*, 49: 370–374.

Grolnick, S. (1990). *The Work and Play of Winnicott*. Northvale, NJ: Jason Aronson.

Grolnick, S. A., Barkin, L., & Muensterberger, W. (Eds.) (1978). *Between Reality and Fantasy: Transitional Objects and Phenomena*. New York: International Universities Press.

Gull, W. W. (1874). Apepsia hysterica: anorexia hysterica. *Transcripts of the Clinical Society of London*, 7: 22–28.

Guntrip, H. (1975). My experience of analysis with Fairbairn and Winnicott (how complete a result does psycho-analytic therapy achieve?). *International Review of Psycho-Analysis*, 2: 145–156.

Hale, R., & Sinason, V. (1994). Internal and external reality: establishing parameters. In: V. Sinason (Ed.), *Treating Survivors of Satanist Abuse* (pp. 274–284). London: Routledge.

Huizinga, J. (1949). *Homo Ludens: A Study of the Play-Element in Culture*. London: Routledge & Kegan Paul.

Jacobs, M. (1995). *D. W. Winnicott*. London: Sage Publications.

Jacobson, E. (1946). The effect of disappointment on ego and superego function in normal and depressive development. *Psychoanalytic Review*, 32: 255–262.

Jones, E. (1957). *Sigmund Freud: Life and Work. Vol. Three: The Last Years, 1919–1939*. London: Hogarth Press.

Kahr, B. (1991). The sexual molestation of children: historical perspectives. *Journal of Psychohistory, 19*: 191–214.

Kahr, B. (1996a). *D. W. Winnicott: A Biographical Portrait*. London: Karnac Books.

Kahr, B. (1996b). Donald Winnicott and the foundations of child psychotherapy. *Journal of Child Psychotherapy, 22*, 327–342.

Kahr, B. (1998). An unpublished fragment by Donald Winnicott. *NewSquiggle, 2*: 7.

Kahr, B. (1999). Sigmund Freud and the case of the paedophile. *Psychotherapy Review, 1*: 89–90.

Kahr, B. (2000). Donald Woods Winnicott: the cartographer of infancy. In: B. Kahr (Ed.), *The Legacy of Winnicott: Essays on Infant and Child Mental Health*, London: Karnac Books.

Kahr, B. (in preparation). "Psychoanalysis and Paedophilia: The Psychodynamics of Young Sex Offenders."

Kernberg, O. (1975). *Borderline Conditions and Pathological Narcissism*. New York: Jason Aronson.

Kestenberg, J. S. (1956). On the development of maternal feelings in early childhood. *Psychoanalytic Study of the Child, 11*: 257–291.

Kestenberg, J. S. (1970). "Discussion of Greenacre: 'The Transitional Object and the Fetish: Special Reference to the Role of Illusion'." New York Psychoanalytic Society, New York (17 March).

Kestenberg, J. S., & Weinstein, J. (1988). Transitional objects and body-image formation. In: S. A. Grolnick, L. Barkin, & W. Muensterberger (Eds.), *Between Reality and Phantasy: Transitional Objects and Phenomena* (pp. 75–97). New York: Jason Aronson.

Klein, M. (1946). Notes on some schizoid mechanisms. *International Journal of Psycho-Analysis, 27*: 99–110.

Kohut, H. (1971). *The Analysis of the Self: A Systematic Approach to the Psychoanalytic Treatment of Narcissistic Personality Disorders*. New York: International Universities Press.

Krueger, D. W. (1988). Body self, psychological self, and bulimia: developmental and clinical considerations. In: H. J. Schwartz (Ed.), *Bulimia: Psychoanalytic Treatment and Theory* (pp. 55–73). Madison, CT: International Universities Press.

Lampl-de Groot, J. (1946). The preoedipal phase in the development of the male child. *Psychoanalytic Study of the Child, 2*: 75–112.

Little, M. I. (1985). Winnicott working in areas where psychotic anxieties predominate: a personal record. *Free Associations, 1* (3): 9–42.

Mahler, M. S. (1966). Notes on the development of basic moods: the depressive affect. In: R. M. Loewenstein, L. M. Newman, M. Schur, & A. J. Solnit (Eds.), *Psychoanalysis: A General Psychology. Essays in Honor of Heinz Hartmann* (pp. 152–168). New York: International Universities Press.

Mahler, M. S. (1968). *On Human Symbiosis and the Vicissitudes of Individuation*. New York: International Universities Press.

Mahler, M. S. (1974). Symbiosis and individuation: the psychological birth of the human infant. *Psychoanalytic Study of the Child, 29*: 89–106.

Mahler, M. S., & Furer, M. (1968). *On Human Symbiosis and the Vicissitudes of Individuation*. New York: International Universities Press.

Mahler, M. S., Pine, F., & Bergman, A. (1975). *The Psychological Birth of the Human Infant: Symbiosis and Individuation*. New York: Basic Books.

McDougall, J. (1980). *Plea for a Measure of Abnormality*. New York: International Universities Press.

McDougall, J. (1989). *Theatres of the Body: A Psychoanalytic Approach to Psychosomatic Illness*. London: Free Association Books.

McDougall, J. (1995). *The Many Faces of Eros*. London: Free Association Books.

Moore, B. E., & Fine, B. D. (1990). *Psychoanalytic Terms and Concepts*. New Haven, CT: Yale University Press.

Murray, L. (1991). Intersubjectivity, object relations theory, and empirical evidence from mother–infant interactions. *Infant Mental Health Journal, 12*: 219–232.

Natterson, J. M. (1966). Theodor Reik: masochism in modern man. In: F. Alexander, S. Eisenstein, & M. Grotjahn (Eds.), *Psychoanalytic Pioneers* (pp. 249–264). New York: Basic Books.

Novick, J. (1976). Termination of treatment in adolescence. *Psychoanalytic Study of the Child, 31*: 389–414.

Parker, R. (1994). Maternal Ambivalence. *Winnicott Studies, Vol. 9* (pp. 3–17). London: Karnac Books.

Phillips, A. (1988). *Winnicott*. London: Fontana.

Phillips, A. (1993). Contingency for beginners. *Winnicott Studies, Vol. 8* (pp. 31–45). London: Karnac Books.

Prall, R. C. (1978). The role of the father in the preoedipal years. *Journal of the American Psychoanalytic Association, 27*: 143–161.

Raphael-Leff, J. (1985). Facilitators and regulators: vulnerability to postnatal disturbance. *Journal of Psychosomatic Obstetrics and Gynaecology, 4*: 151–168.

Raphael-Leff, J. (1986). Facilitators and regulators: conscious and unconscious processes in pregnancy and early motherhood. *British Journal of Medical Psychology 59*: 43–55.

Raphael-Leff, J. (1991). *Psychological Processes of Childbearing*. London: Chapman & Hall.

Raphael-Leff, J. (1993). *Pregnancy: The Inside Story*. London: Sheldon Press.

Raphael-Leff, J. (1994). Imaginative bodies of childbearing: visions and revisions. In: A. Erskine & D. Judd (Eds.). *The Imaginative Body: Psychodynamic Therapy in Health Care* (pp. 13–42). London: Whurr Publishers.

Raphael-Leff, J. (1995). Narcissistic displacement in childbearing. In: J. Cooper & N. Maxwell (Eds.), *Narcissistic Wounds: British Perspectives on Narcissism* (pp. 77–93). London: Whurr Publishers.

Raphael-Leff, J. (1996). Reproductive narratives of pregnancy and parenting. In: C. Clulow (Ed.), *Partners Becoming Parents: Talks from the Tavistock Marital Studies Institute* (pp. 66–85). London: Sheldon Press.

Rascovsky, A., & Rascovsky, M. (1968). Genesis and acting out of psychopathic behaviour in Sophocles' *Oedipus*: notes on filicide. *International Journal of Psycho-Analysis, 49*: 390–394.

Reiser, L. W. (1990). The oral triad and the bulimic quintet: understanding the bulimic episode. *International Review of Psycho-Analysis, 17*: 238–248.

Rizzuto, A.-M. (1988). Transference, language, and affect in the treatment of bulimarexia. *International Journal of Psycho-Analysis, 69*: 369–387.

Rodgers, A. T. (1979). *The Universal Drum: Dance Imagery in the Poetry of Eliot, Crane, Roethke and Williams*. University Park, PA: Pennsylvania State University Press.

Rorschach, H. (1921). *Psychodiagnostik*. Bern: Verlag Hans Huber.

Rosenberg, E. (1943). A clinical contribution to the psychopathology of the war neuroses. *International Journal of Psycho-Analysis, 24*: 32–41.

Siegelman, E. (1990). *Metaphor and Meaning in Psychotherapy*. New York: Guilford Press.

Sinason, V. (1988a). Smiling, swallowing, sickening and stupefying: the effect of sexual abuse on the child. *Psychoanalytic Psychotherapy, 3*: 97–111.

Sinason, V. (1988b). Dolls and bears: from symbolic equation to symbol. The significance of different play material for sexually abused children and others. *British Journal of Psychotherapy, 4*: 349–363.

Sinason, V. (1992). *Mental Handicap and the Human Condition: New Approaches from the Tavistock*. London: Free Association Books.

Sinason, V., & Svensson, A. (1994). Going through the fifth window: "Other cases rest on Sundays. This one didn't." In: V. Sinason (Ed.), *Treating Survivors of Satanist Abuse* (pp. 13–21). London: Routledge.

Socarides, C. W. (1960). The development of a fetishistic perversion: the contribution of preoedipal phase conflict. *Journal of the American Psychoanalytic Association, 8:* 281–311.

Socarides, C. W. (1974). Homosexuality. In: S. Arieti (Ed.), *The American Handbook of Psychiatry, Vol. 3: Adult Clinical Psychiatry* (2nd edition, pp. 291–315). New York: Basic Books.

Socarides, C. W. (1978). *Homosexuality*. New York: Jason Aronson.

Socarides, C. W. (1980). Homosexuality and the rapprochement subphase crisis. In: R. F. Lax, S. Bach, & J. A. Burland (Eds.), *Rapprochement: A Critical Subphase in Separation-Individuation* (pp. 331–352). New York: Jason Aronson.

Socarides, C. W. (1982). Abdicating fathers, homosexual sons: psychoanalytic observations on the contribution of the father to the development of male homosexuality. In: S. H. Cath, A. R. Gurwith, & J. M. Ross (Eds.), *Father and Child: Development and Clinical Perspectives* (pp. 509–521). Boston, MA: Little, Brown.

Socarides, C. W. (1985). Depression in perversion: with special reference to the function of erotic experience in sexual perversions. In: V. D. Volkan (Ed.), *Depressive States and Their Treatment* (pp. 317–334). New York: Jason Aronson.

Socarides, C. W. (1988). *The Preoedipal Origin and Psychoanalytic Therapy of Sexual Perversions*. Madison, CT: International Universities Press.

Socarides, D. D., & Stolorow, R. D. (1985). Affects and selfobjects. *Annual of Psychoanalysis, 12–13:* 105–119.

Sperling, M. (1949). The role of the mother in psychsomatic disorders in children. *Psychosomatic Medicine, 11:* 377–385.

Sperling, M. (1959). A study of deviate sexual behavior in children by the method of simultaneous analysis of mother and child. In: L. Jessner & E. Pavenstedt (Eds.), *Dynamic Psychopathology in Childhood* (pp. 221–243). New York: Grune & Stratton.

Sperling, M. (1963). Fetishism in children. *Psychoanalytic Quarterly, 32:* 374–392.

Sperling, M. (1964). The analysis of a boy with transvestite tendencies: a contribution to the genesis and dynamics of tranvestism. *Psychoanalytic Study of the Child, 19:* 470–493.

Sperling, O. (1944). On appersonation. *International Journal of Psycho-Analysis, 25*: 128–132.

Spitz, R. (1959). *The Genetic Field Theory of Ego Formation.* New York: International Universities Press.

States, B. O. (1978). *The Shape of Paradox: An Essay on Waiting for Godot.* Berkeley, CA: University of California Press.

Sterba, R. (1934). The fate of the ego in analytic therapy. *International Journal of Psycho-Analysis, 15*: 117–126.

Stern, D. N. (1974). The goal and structure of mother–infant play. *Journal of the American Academy of Child Psychiatry, 13*: 402–421.

Stern, D. N. (1985). *The Interpersonal World of the Infant: A View from Psychoanalysis and Developmental Psychology.* New York: Basic Books.

Stern, D. N. (1994). One way to build a clinically relevant baby. *Infant Mental Health Journal 15*: 9–25.

Stoller, R. J. (1968). *Sex and Gender, Vol. 1.* New York: Science House.

Stoller, R. J. (1975a). *Perversion: The Erotic Form of Hatred.* New York: Pantheon.

Stoller, R. J. (1975b). Healthy parental influences on the earliest development of masculinity in baby boys. *Psychoanalytic Forum, 5*: 234–240.

Stoller, R. J. (1991). The term *perversion.* In: G. Fogel & W. Myers (Eds.), *Perversions and Near-Perversions in Clinical Practice: New Psychoanalytic Perspectives* (pp. 36–56). New Haven, CT: Yale University Press.

Trevarthen, C. (1979). Communication and cooperation in early infancy: a description of primary intersubjectivity. In: M. Bullowa (Ed.), *Before Speech: The Beginning of Interpersonal Communication* (pp. 321–327). Cambridge: Cambridge University Press.

Tronick, E. Z., & Gianino, A. F. (1986). Interactive mismatch and repair: challenges to the coping infant. *Zero to Three, 4*: 1–6.

van der Leeuw, P. J. (1958). The preoedipal phase of the male. *Psychoanalytic Study of the Child, 13*: 352–374.

Volkan, V. D. (1981). *Linking Objects and Linking Phenomena: A Study of Forms, Symptoms, Metapsychology, and Therapy of Complicated Mourning.* New York: International Universities Press.

Volkan, V. D. (1988). *The Need to Have Enemies and Allies: From Clinical Practice to International Relationships.* Northvale, NJ: Jason Aronson.

Volkan, V. D. (1995). *The Infantile Psychotic Self and Its Fates: Understanding and Treating Schizophrenics and Other Difficult Patients.* Northvale, NJ: Jason Aronson.

Volkan, V. D. (1997). *Bloodlines: From Ethnic Pride to Ethnic Terrorism.* New York: Farrar, Straus & Giroux.

Volkan, V. D. (1999). *Das Versagen der Diplomatie: Zur Psychoanalyse nationaler, ethnischer und religiöser Konflikte* [The Failure of Diplomacy: The Psychoanalysis of National, Ethnic and Religious Conflicts]. Giessen: Psychosozial-Verlag.

Volkan, V. D., & Zintl, E. (1993). *Life after Loss: Lessons of Grief.* New York: Charles Scribner's Sons.

Vygotsky, L. S. (1962). *Thought and Language,* ed. and trans. E. Haufman & G. Vakar. Cambridge, MA: M.I.T. Press.

Welldon, E. V. (1988). *Mother, Madonna, Whore: The Idealization and Denigration of Motherhood.* London: Free Association Books.

Werner, H., & Kaplan, B. (1963). *Symbol Formation.* New York: Wiley.

Winnicott, C. (1978). D.W.W.: a reflection. In: S. A. Grolnick, L. Barkin, & W. Muensterberger (Eds.), *Between Reality and Fantasy: Transitional Objects and Phenomena* (pp. 17–33). New York: Jason Aronson.

Winnicott, C. (1984). Introduction. In: D. W. Winnicott, *Deprivation and Delinquency* (pp. 1–5), ed. C. Winnicott, R. Shepherd, & M. Davis. London: Tavistock Publications.

Winnicott, D. W. (1931). *Clinical Notes on Disorders of Childhood.* London: Heinemann Medical.

Winnicott, D. W. (1935). The manic defence. In: *Collected Papers: Through Paediatrics to Psycho-Analysis* (pp. 129–144). London: Tavistock Publications, 1958.

Winnicott, D. W. (1941). The observation of infants in a set situation. In: *Collected Papers: Through Paediatrics to Psycho-Analysis* (pp. 52–69). London: Tavistock Publications, 1958.

Winnicott, D. W. (1943). Delinquency research. *The New Era in Home and School, 24,* 65–67.

Winnicott, D. W. (1945). The evacuated child. In: *The Child and the Outside World: Studies in Developing Relationships* (pp. 83–87), ed. J. Hardenberg. London: Tavistock Publications, 1957.

Winnicott, D. W. (1948a). Children's hostels in war and peace: a contribution to the symposium on "Lessons for child psychiatry". (Given at a meeting of the Medical Section of the British Psychological Society, 27 February 1946.) *British Journal of Medical Psychology, 21,* 175–180.

Winnicott, D. W. (1948b). Letter to Anna Freud, 6th July. In: *The Spontaneous Gesture: Selected Letters of D. W. Winnicott* (pp. 10–12), ed. F. R. Rodman. Cambridge, MA: Harvard University Press, 1987.

Winnicott, D. W. (1949a) Hate in the counter-transference. *International Journal of Psycho-Analysis: 30*: 69–74.

Winnicott, D. W. (1949b). Letter to the Editor of *The Times*, 10th August. In: *The Spontaneous Gesture: Selected Letters of D. W. Winnicott* (pp. 15–16), ed. F.R. Rodman. Cambridge, MA: Harvard University Press, 1987.

Winnicott, D. W. (1949c). Letter to R. S. Hazlehurst, 1st September. In: *The Spontaneous Gesture: Selected Letters of D. W. Winnicott* (p. 17), ed. F. R. Rodman. Cambridge, MA: Harvard University Press, 1987.

Winnicott, D. W. (1949d). Letter to S. H. Hodge, 1st September. In: *The Spontaneous Gesture: Selected Letters of D. W. Winnicott* (pp. 17–19), ed. F. R. Rodman. Cambridge, MA: Harvard University Press, 1987.

Winnicott, D. W. (1950a). Aggression in relation to emotional development. In: D. W. Winnicott, *Collected Papers: Through Paediatrics to Psycho-Analysis* (pp. 204–218). London: Tavistock Publications, 1958.

Winnicott, D. W. (1950b). Letter to P. D. Scott, 11th May. In: *The Spontaneous Gesture: Selected Letters of D. W. Winnicott* (pp. 22–23), ed. F. R. Rodman. Cambridge, MA: Harvard University Press, 1987.

Winnicott, D. W. (1952). Letter to Melanie Klein, 17th November. In: *The Spontaneous Gesture: Selected Letters of D. W. Winnicott* (pp. 33–37), ed. F. R. Rodman. Cambridge, MA: Harvard University Press, 1987.

Winnicott, D. W. (1953a). Transitional objects and transitional phenomena: a study of the first not-me possession. *International Journal of Psycho-Analysis, 34*: 89–97.

Winnicott, D. W. (1953b). Letter to W. Clifford M. Scott, 19th March. In: *The Spontaneous Gesture: Selected Letters of D. W. Winnicott* (pp. 48–49), ed. F. R. Rodman. Cambridge, MA: Harvard University Press, 1987.

Winnicott, D. W. (1954). Mind and its relation to the psyche-soma. *British Journal of Medical Psychology, 27*: 201–209.

Winnicott, D. W. (1956a). Primary maternal preoccupation. In: *Collected Papers: Through Paediatrics to Psycho-Analysis* (pp. 300–305). London: Tavistock Publications, 1958.

Winnicott, D. W. (1956b). The antisocial tendency. In: D. W. Winnicott, *Collected Papers: Through Paediatrics to Psycho-Analysis* (pp. 306–315). London: Tavistock Publications, 1958.

Winnicott, D. W. (1958a). Psycho-analysis and the sense of guilt. In: J. D. Sutherland (Ed.), *Psycho-Analysis and Contemporary Thought* (pp. 15–32). London: Tavistock Publications.

Winnicott, D. W. (1958b). The capacity to be alone. *International Journal of Psycho-Analysis, 39*: 416–420.

Winnicott, D. W. (1960a). String. *Journal of Child Psychology and Psychiatry and Allied Disciplines, 1*: 49–52.

Winnicott, D. W. (1960b). The theory of the parent–infant relationship. *International Journal of Psycho-Analysis, 41*: 585–595.

Winnicott, D. W. (1960c). Ego distortion in terms of true and false self. In: *The Maturational Processes and the Facilitating Environment: Studies in the Theory of Emotional Development* (pp. 140–152). London: Hogarth Press & The Institute of Psycho-Analysis, 1965.

Winnicott, D. W. (1961a). Comments on the *Report of the Committee on Punishment in Prisons and Borstals.* In: *Deprivation and Delinquency* (pp. 202–208), ed. C. Winnicott, R. Shepherd, & M. Davis. London: Tavistock Publications, 1984.

Winnicott, D. W. (1961b). Varieties of psychotherapy. In: *Deprivation and Delinquency* (pp. 232–240), ed. C. Winnicott, R. Shepherd, & M. Davis. London: Tavistock Publications, 1984.

Winnicott, D. W. (1962). Ego integration in child development. In: *The Maturational Processes and the Facilitating Environment: Studies in the Theory of Emotional Development* (pp. 56–63). London: Hogarth Press & The Institute of Psycho-Analysis, 1965.

Winnicott, D. W. (1963a). Dependence in infant care, in child care, and in the psycho-analytic setting. *International Journal of Psycho-Analysis, 44*: 339–344.

Winnicott, D. W. (1963b). Communicating and not communicating leading to a study of certain opposites. In: *The Maturational Processes and the Facilitating Environment: Studies in the Theory of Emotional Development* (pp. 179–192). London: Hogarth Press & The Institute of Psycho-Analysis, 1965.

Winnicott, D. W. (1963c). Psychotherapy of character disorders. In: *The Maturational Processes and the Facilitating Environment: Studies in the Theory of Emotional Development* (pp. 203–216). London: Hogarth Press & The Institute of Psycho-Analysis, 1965.

Winnicott, D. W. (1963d). Psychiatric disorder in terms of infantile maturational processes. In: *The Maturational Processes and the Facilitating Environment: Studies in the Theory of Emotional Development* (pp. 230–241). London: Hogarth Press & The Institute of Psycho-Analysis, 1965.

Winnicott, D. W. (1963e). Hospital care supplementing intensive psychotherapy in adolescence. In: *The Maturational Processes and the Facilitating Environment: Studies in the Theory of Emotional Development* (pp. 242–248). London: Hogarth Press & The Institute of Psycho-Analysis, 1965.

Winnicott, D. W. (1965). The price of disregarding psychoanalytic research. In: *Home Is Where We Start From: Essays by a Psychoanalyst* (pp. 172–182), ed. C. Winnicott, R. Shepherd, & M. Davis. Harmondsworth, Middlesex: Penguin Books, 1986.

Winnicott, D. W. (1967). The location of cultural experience. *International Journal of Psycho-Analysis, 48*: 368–372.

Winnicott, D. W. (1968). Delinquency as a sign of hope. *Prison Service Journal, 7*: 2–9.

Winnicott, D. W. (1969a). Letter to J. D. Collinson, 10 March. In: *The Spontaneous Gesture: Selected Letters of D. W. Winnicott* (pp. 186–188), ed. F.R. Rodman. Cambridge, MA: Harvard University Press, 1987.

Winnicott, D. W. (1969b). Letter to Richard Balbernie, 18 March. Box 7, File 10, Donald W. Winnicott Papers, Archives of Psychiatry, History of Psychiatry Section, Department of Psychiatry. The Oskar Diethelm Library of the History of Psychiatry, The New York Hospital, Cornell Medical Center, New York, NY.

Winnicott, D. W. (1970). "A Personal Statement about Dynamic Psychology." Unpublished typescript, Winnicott Trust, London.

Winnicott, D. W. (1971). *Playing and Reality*. London: Tavistock Publications.

Winnicott, D. W. (1974). Fear of breakdown. *International Review of Psycho-Analysis, 1*: 103–107.

Winnicott, D. W. (1984). *Deprivation and Delinquency*, ed. C. Winnicott, R. Shepherd, & M. Davis. London: Tavistock Publications.

Winnicott, D. W. (1987). *The Spontaneous Gesture: Selected Letters of D. W. Winnicott*, ed. F. R. Rodman. Cambridge, MA: Harvard University Press.

Winnicott, D. W. (1988). *Human Nature*, ed. C. Bollas, M. Davis, & R. Shepherd. London: Free Association Books.

Winnicott, D. W., & Britton, C. (1944). The problem of homeless children. *The New Era in Home and School, 25*: 155–161.

Winnicott, D. W., & Britton, C. (1947). Residential management as treatment for difficult children: the evolution of a wartime hostels scheme. *Human Relations, 1*: 87–97.

# INDEX

Abelin, E. L., 102
active feminine pre-oedipal
        identification, 97
"Adam" [case study], 48–49
Adelson, E., 49
adolescence, psychopathology of,
        61–71
adolescent forensic patient, 51–60
aesthetic imperative, 119
Albert Einstein College of
        Medicine, New York City,
        xv
alcoholism [case study], 91
Allgemeines Krankenhaus, Vienna,
        2
ambivalence, 52
    maternal, 35–40
Anna Freud Centre, London, xiii
anorexia, 10, 77, 79
arson, 2, 55
"as-if" character [case study], 88–90
Association of Child Psychology
        and Psychiatry, 16

attachment, symbiotic, 89
attunement, 107
    mother–infant, 15, 31
autonomy, 35, 55, 88, 89, 96

baby(ies) as transitional object(s),
        19–25, 117
Bachelard, G., 120
Balbernie, R., 8
Barkin, L., xx
Barth, K., 122
beating experiences, Freud on, 3
"Beatrice" [case study], 48–49
Beebe, B., 31
Bergman, A., 30, 95
Bertin, C., x
Bibring, E., 107
body:
    -ego image, 97
    image, 75, 77
    products, as intermediate
        objects, 74
Bonaparte, M., x

process, transitional, xx
projection(s), 41, 43, 53
projective identification, 33, 35, 57,
        84, 113
projective mechanisms, 84
pseudo-hallucination(s), 32
pseudo-normality, xxii, 9, 61–71
psychic synthesis, 88
psychopathology, xxii, 8, 22, 83–86,
        90–94, 96, 106, 117, 121
    of adolescence, 61–71
    of criminology, 7
    forensic, 7
psychosexual development, stages
        of, 85
psychosis, 10
psychotherapy, forensic, *see*
        forensic psychotherapy
pyromania, 2

Rank, O., x
Raphael-Leff, J., xv, 9, 27–41
Rascovsky, A., 46
Rascovsky, M., 46
Regent's College, London, ix
    School of Psychotherapy and
        Counselling, xiv
Reik, T., 2
Reiser, L. W., 73
relatedness, transitional, xx
resistance(s), 21, 46, 61, 62, 120
Rilke, R. M., 43
Rizzuto, A.-M., 80
Robinson, H. Taylor, xiv
Rodgers, A. T., 119
Rorschach, H., 115
Rosen, I., xi
Rosenberg, E., 5
Royal College of Psychiatrists,
        U.K., xiii, xv, 1
Royal Society of Medicine, 15

Sachs, H., x
sadism, 58, 90, 104, 105, 108, 109
sadomasochism, 80, 101
"Sammy" [case study], 53–56

satanist abuse, 9, 48
schizophrenia, 90, 92
Schmideberg, M., xi
Scott, P. D., 7
secondary identification, 98
separation:
    anxiety, 103, 107
    –individuation, 23, 57, 85–88, 94–
        96, 98–100, 102
Shakespeare, W., 113–116, 120
Shapiro, V., 49
Shepherd, R., xiv, 16
Siegelman, E., 112
Sinason, V., xv, 9, 43–49
Socarides, C. W., xv, 10, 95–109
Socarides, D. D., 107
space, transitional, *see* transitional
        space
Sperling, M., 22, 74
Spitz, R., 95, 96, 99, 107
splitting, 35, 37, 41
squiggle, xxi, 111, 113, 115, 120, 121
    game, 16
Squiggle Foundation, xiv
St. Bartholomew's Hospital,
        London, xi, 3
St. George's Hospital Medical
        School, London, xv
States, B. O., 115
Sterba, R., 84
Stern, D. N., 31, 62, 63
"Steven" [case study], 44–46, 49
Stoller, R. J., 23, 24, 25, 104, 105
Stolorow, R. D., 107
Strachey, J., 3, 12
"suitable reservoirs" [Volkan], xxi
superego, 38
    functioning, pathological
        development of, 22
Svensson, A., 48
symbiosis, 85–94
    mother–infant, 23
symbiotic attachment, 89
symbiotic fusion, mother–infant,
        85, 90, 94
symbolism, xxi

"we meanings" [Vygotsky], 63
Werner, H., xxi
Westwick, A., ix, x, xi
whole object relationship, 73, 74, 81
Wilde, O., 49
Williams, W. C., 119
Winnicott, C. Britton, 4, 13, 16
Winnicott, D. W., *passim*
  on dangerousness, 1–10
  on delinquency as sign of hope, 6, 8, 51, 60
  on good-enough mother, 52
  "graduated failure of adaptation", 31
  on intrauterine environment, 28
  on maternal ambivalence, 35
  on maternal holding, 34
on playing, xxi
on primary maternal preoccupation, 30–31
role of, in forensic psychotherapy, 111–123
on sexual perversions, 95–109
"there is no such thing as a baby", 27, 95
on transitional objects, 74, 83
on transitional space, 83, 85
on transitional states, 85
Winnicott Clinic of Psychotherapy, xiv
Winnicott Publications Committee, xiv, 9
Winnicott Trust, xiv, 9, 16

Zintl, E., xxi